ANIMAIL

Windmill Books, Inc.

and E. P. Dutton & Co., Inc.

New York

ANIMAIL

Cleveland Amory

Introduction by Mary Tyler Moore

Drawings by Robert Kraus

LIBRARY OF CONGRESS CATALOGING IN PUBLICATION DATA

Amory, Cleveland. Animail
1. Zoology—Miscellanea. 2. Pets—Miscellanea.
I. Title.
QL50.A46   1976   596   76-21692
ISBN: 0-525-61558-X

Published simultaneously in Canada by
Clarke, Irwin & Company, Limited, Toronto and Vancouver

Designed by The Etheredges

Printed in the U.S.A. First Edition

10 9 8 7 6 5 4 3 2 1

For Marian Probst,
who pioneered it as a column,
and for Paula Deats,
whose contributions helped make it a book.

Contents

Introduction by
Mary Tyler Moore

I grew up in a small house in Brooklyn, and though my family was neither rich nor poor, we were definitely "city." Consequently, I used to love visits to my grandparents' home in Virginia. They were "country." Once there, I'd head for my favorite room—a great woodsy den that was my grandfather's trophy room. Like most children, I was fascinated with animals, and this room was filled with them. The walls were covered with stuffed heads of bears, deer, wolves, even birds. My grandfather would lift me up to touch them. I petted them and I even named some of them.

Today I can't stand even the idea of such a room. What changed me? My theory is that somewhere along the way, something happens to you about animals and you begin to empathize—a word I love because it really means love—with their suffering. After that you can't look at a fur coat, pillow, rug, or trophy head without stopping to think how it got there.

I was only eight years old when that certain something happened to me about animals. My family had moved to California and we'd been there less than a year when one day on the street I saw a man beating a dog with a stick. Something in me snapped. I ran to the man and started beating him with my fists. I even kicked him—it was almost as if I was trying to do to him what he had been doing to the little dog. The dog ran away and, surprisingly, the man did too. I hit him so hard that I must have really unnerved him. Not only did the incident make me realize the strength of my feelings for animals, it also showed me that sometimes God gives frail, little people superhuman strength. I remember reading about a mother who found the same kind of extraordinary strength when her child was trapped under a car and there was no one else to help. Somehow the woman was able to lift the car single-handedly and free her baby. Though my little story isn't nearly so dramatic, I can understand now how I could have hurt that man enough to make him run from me.

Looking back on my childhood, I can see that my mother was probably the strongest example in setting the course my life has taken. She was into animals as well as show business. In Hollywood she worked on a radio program called "Pet Exchange," where she answered calls on the air from people who wanted to adopt stray dogs that the show rescued from the pound. It was inevitable that the day would come when she couldn't resist bringing one of the strays home herself. Jeff was a beagle mix (with a lot more mix than beagle!), and though I have never known an animal that didn't teach me something, that little dog may have taught me the most of all. He proved what a great pet a mixed breed can be.

My husband, Grant Tinker, is a great animal lover. As a boy he had a dalmatian named Max which he loved dearly and felt so strongly about that we named our first dog after him. Max II was a huge, hulking German shepherd and was usually bossed completely by our other dog, a yelping little poodle named Maude. Maude would bark and snap her orders over and over until finally it would get to be too much for Max. Gently but firmly he'd go over to her and literally take her whole head in his mouth. He wouldn't shake or bite, he'd just hold her until she was quiet. It was as if Max was saying, "Maude, that's enough."

For me, though, just talking about animals has never been enough. By 1971 I had come a long way from my grandfather's trophy room, but up until then I hadn't really done anything to improve the plight of animals. What finally motivated me to become more deeply involved was a film I saw on television one day, narrated by Cleveland Amory, about baby seals and how they are brutally clubbed to death for their fur. I was at our beach house and I remember exactly where I was standing—outside the kitchen door. I also recall just what I was doing—holding a pot of soup.

I am not exactly the flamboyant type, but I got so angry that day that I threw the soup against the wall. Then I called the TV station and they told me how to get in touch with Cleveland. After talking to him, I joined his Fund for Animals.

The Fund is the most active anti-cruelty-to-animals organization in this country and I am very proud to be its national chairman. Now Cleveland has written a book. It's not really about cruelty to animals—although Cleveland pulls no punches about this. It's really a book about what Cleveland finds fascinating about animals—which is pretty nearly everything—in question-and-answer form. I call it Everything-You've-Always-Wanted-to-Know-But-Were-Afraid-To-Ask. And you remember what *that* was about? Well, that's here, too!

If you don't believe it, try his answer to "How do porcupines mate?" or "Can spayed and neutered pets enjoy sex?" It's a book that's both fascinating and fun—yet we can all learn from it, too.

Animal Anomalies

Q. *What does the expression* white elephant *come from? Is there such a thing?* —J. E., GALVESTON, IND.

A. Very rarely—but the point of the expression is how they got to be rarely welcome. In the old days in Siam, any white or "albino" elephant was automatically considered the property of the king—who would then pass the gift on to one of his nobles. However, there was a catch—it was not to a noble who had pleased him; it was to a noble who had displeased him. The expense of looking after the elephant—which, after all, was a gift from the king and therefore had to be cherished—usually broke the noble. In fact, it also broke people in other countries. According to historian Charles Earle Funk, England's Queen Henrietta Maria, who later became something of a white elephant herself, was incensed when her husband, Charles I, received a royal pachyderm. The costs of maintaining him, it seems, were such that the queen was "obliged to put off her visit to Bath, for want of money to bear her charges." She presumably bathed elsewhere.

Q. *Somebody told me animals know what the weather is going to be. Is that true?* —F. F., HINTON, W. VA.

A. My dogs don't even know what the weather *is*—even when I take them to the window, point out the rain, put a few drops on their noses, and try to explain why I can't take them out until later. But cats—ah, cats are a different story. Cats have indeed been known to predict weather. In fact, one, the late Napoleon, owned by a Mrs. Fanny Shields of Baltimore, actually became so famous for his predictions that if they'd had TV weathermen in those days—well, Napoleon certainly would have been the country's first weathercat.

It all began in 1930 when Baltimore had a terrible drought. While all the other forecasters saw no break in the drought, Mrs. Shields called the paper and stated firmly that there would be rain within twenty-four hours. Napoleon, it seems, had assumed his "rain position"—front paws extended and top of head to ground. Anyway, there was rain; and, from then on, the paper regularly published Napoleon's "forecasts." They were amazingly accurate, too. Of course, like other great commentators, Napoleon had his detractors—some people said that his "rain position" was taken simply to seek relief from headaches caused by atmospheric pressures—but Napoleon never dignified such slurs by stooping to comment.

Q. *My boyfriend says Mother Nature is a chauvinist. Do males always run the show in the animal world?* —C. W., BILOXI, MISS.

A. Well, as with humans, it's not that simple. With a few exceptions in the insect and reptile worlds, male animals are generally larger than females and so do enjoy certain advantages by virtue—or perhaps vice—of brute force.

In the cat family, for example, the females are better hunters and do nearly all the family meat-winning—but the males get first crack at the results. On the other hand, in the family of elephants (those superintelligent creatures) the herd leader is a female; mature bulls are admitted to the herd only during brief mating periods.

Many animals, among them eagles, geese and perhaps wolves, mate for life. Some, like ostriches and raccoons, form single family units, and males and females stay together after breeding to share nesting, feeding and rearing duties until the offspring are grown. Others, like chimps, live in multigenerational social groups, and all members help by training, feeding, playing with and even baby-sitting for the young. And, in the pecking order of these groups, there are some dominant females that carry more weight than most of the males.

The life-style of animals is basically not too different from that of humans: males fight over females, and court them and give them gifts to curry their favor. Some males end up with a whole harem of beauties, and some are perpetually rejected. Female bighorn sheep, for example, will brook no incompetence in their suitors, while wolf packs have been known to have plenty of jealous lovers and even triangles, quadrangles and pentagles.

Q. *What does the phrase* charley horse *come from? Why horse?* —E. VW., CORONA DEL MAR. CALIF.

A. You sent me to the library on that one. But darned if the expression doesn't indeed come from a horse. Back in the good old days, the late 80s and early 90s, there was a horse named Charley who pulled a roller around to lay the infield dust at the Chicago White Sox ballpark. And Charley had a peculiar limp. In no time at all, ballplayers who pulled up lame were said to have Charley horses. Why was Charley lame? Listen, one question to a customer.

Q. *Can animals learn to understand more than one language? Do animals in different countries "speak" different languages?* —C. T., RAY-VILLE, LA.

A. But of course. There are numerous instances of diplomatic pets, for example, that have learned to respond to commands in more than one language from bilingual and sometimes trilingual masters, and there also are numerous circus stories of individual animals that would, say, obey a command given in English before they would respond to one in German, although they understood the command in both languages.

According to Barry Farber, New York's great late-night broadcaster who himself speaks eleven languages, animals in different countries do, at the very least, "make different sounds." Dogs in Sweden, according to Farber, say not "bow wow" but "vov vov," while their counterparts across the border in Finland don't say either; they say "hau hau." Imagine two dachshunds meeting at the Swedish-Finnish border, one saying "vov vov," the other "hau hau." A thing like that could start a war. Nor does this stop with domestic animals. Pigs in the United States who say "oink" would be puzzled to meet their Scandinavian counterparts who, for some reason, say "nuunk." And even roosters who, as we all know, in this country say "cock-a-doodle-do," say, in Norway, "kukukulu."

There is, however, a certain New York City French teacher—a cat lover—who firmly believes that all cats, no matter what their "native" language is, would prefer to be spoken to only in French. "French," she says, "is a much more elegant language—as cats themselves are elegant. It has the nasal tones that appeal to cats. Instinctively, most cats are at home with it."

According to Farber, cats don't speak French, or English, or anything else—they speak "cat." Cats everywhere, he says, say "meow." To which we say both "hau hau" and "nuunk." The two cats we know best have never said "meow" in their lives. One says a very distinct "bur-durp," and the other says, plainly, "Frank." His name, incidentally, is Timothy.

Q. Do animals have a sense of time? My dog gives me almost as much of a welcome when I've been down the block to the drugstore as he does when I've been gone for a week. —F. R., CHATTANOOGA, TENN.

A. They do not have the same sense of time we do, and be glad of it. If they did, can you imagine what it would be like for a dog to wait all day for his "person"—say, a young boy—to come home? Remember, all day for the dog is a sizable part of his short life. And then the boy comes home and maybe something has gone wrong at school or on the way home, and he ignores the dog or goes right to the kitchen or his room. The dog's whole life would be crushed.

Be thankful they don't have a good sense of time. It's one of the few good breaks in their often sad lives.

Q. Can animals talk to each other telepathically? —T. D., EAST LIVERPOOL, OHIO.

A. Well, if it isn't telepathy, I don't know what you'd call it. If you don't believe it, and you have more than one pet, put one in one room and one in another. I guarantee that whatever you do or even say to one will be known to the other—and before they can get back together. Writer Ronald Porep recently described how animals can predict earthquakes. He said that after the San Francisco earthquake people recalled the strange snorting of horses—well before any humans knew anything was wrong. And when Hawaii had a volcanic eruption in the winter of '66, the night before it the dogs on the island acted very strangely. "They ran around excitedly," said Porep, "and dug holes in the ground." Two psychologists at the University of Chicago, the Drs. Anderson, have collected much data on the subject, including the fact that people who live near Mount Etna of Vesuvius fame literally go by their cats. When their cats run out of their houses, so do the people. All I can say is they must make a lot of unnecessary trips.

Q. *Do you believe in ESP between people and animals?* —M. P., SEATTLE, WASH.

A. I do believe in ESP between animals and persons, because some people really do have an inexplicably extraordinary ability to communicate with animals. I give you the example of a young woman named Beatrice Lydecker of Los Angeles.

"In 1968," she told me, "I wanted desperately to begin to do something constructive with my life. Almost immediately somebody gave me a book called *Kinship with All Life*.

"One day I was walking along the street in Monrovia, California, thinking about the book, and I stopped to pat a German shepherd in a yard. He looked something like my shepherd who had just died. And as I patted him, I suddenly realized I knew exactly what he was thinking."

What, I wanted to know, was he thinking? "He was lonely, blue and upset," she said. "He told me it was the first time in his life he had ever been left by himself." Later Ms. Lydecker learned that his owner had been in an auto accident, after which he had gotten the dog, and that very day, after recuperating, he had gone back to work.

What did Ms. Lydecker tell the dog? "I didn't tell the dog

anything. I told the owner he would have to get another dog as a companion for the first. He did, too—and everything was all right."

Ms. Lydecker's next case was a Doberman pinscher on guard duty. "That dog was upset, too. He was lonely and unhappy." Ms. Lydecker couldn't do anything about it, but she became even more determined to develop her communication ability with animals.

Her third case was a horse who had been treated for a bad leg for nine months but couldn't seem to get well. "They were going to put the horse down; he couldn't even step on the leg."

"I spoke to the horse," she said, "and he told me he wasn't really sick—his leg wasn't really injured and he just didn't want to get well. He knew that if he recovered he would have to go back to his hated old owner who had mistreated him. He liked the people who were keeping him, and would rather have died than go back to his real owner." This time Ms. Lydecker persuaded the people who were keeping the horse to buy him.

After that case, she started charging for her work. She has been doing it now for six years, and charges twenty dollars an hour. It usually takes her no more than two visits per animal problem.

A particularly difficult case was one involving a large shepherd-Samoyed mix owned by a friend named Bonnie. Every May Bonnie's dog went berserk; he would not stay away from her. If she let him out, the dog would do anything to get back to her, including climbing to the roof and breaking into an upper-story window. Then, after the month of May ended, he was fine. This went on for four years.

How did Ms. Lydecker figure that one out? "I didn't figure it out," she answered indignantly. "The dog told me. The dog told me that he was afraid Bonnie would go away." Later, sure as shooting, Ms. Lydecker found out that in the past Bonnie had indeed gone away on long trips every May for four years.

How, I persisted, did the dog tell her?

"I see," she said, "mental pictures."

"Most animal problems are emotional," Ms. Lydecker continued. "Why does an animal scratch? It scratches because it's upset. Why does an animal wet? It wets because it's trying to eliminate something."

That, I agreed, really did figure. Ms. Lydecker ignored me. One lady, she said, had two cats who were always spraying her furniture. "I asked them which one was doing it. Right away, the guilty one admitted it to me."

This was too much.

"The one who is doing it *always* admits it," Ms. Lydecker said sternly. "Animals are very honest if you ask them directly about something."

Is that true? I suggest you ask your cat.

Q. *Do you believe astrology applies to animals?* —M. F., ELIZABETH CITY, N.DAK.

A. I'll be open to anything, even astrology, if it includes animals in its beliefs. And just because of your letter, I made an effort to have a visit with the country's number one animal astrologer.

Yes, there is one. Her name is Dorothy MacDonald, and she

lives in Los Angeles. She is a charming little woman in her eighties, who is about five feet tall, "With," she says, "my heels."

Ms. MacDonald got into astrology as a kid in school, "First with people," she says, "but then with pets, too."

She's authored a book on the subject, and my first suspicion that I was going to have some trouble here was when she told me that her editor on the book had been Midge, her black cat.

"Midge was a stray, but I know she was born in August. That means she's a Leo. You can see what a showman she is—Leos are great showmen. Look at that picture of her lying on my typewriter.

"Now take my dog, Buffie," Ms. MacDonald continued. "She is a mixture of spaniel and schnauzer. Buffie was born in November, so she is a little Scorpio. She's very sensitive, very introverted, very secretive. But Scorpios make the best detectives, you know. Buffie is very intuitive—very good at finding things."

What signs, I asked, make difficult pets? "Virgo," she said fiercely. "They are so peculiar and analytical. Very critical, too."

I told her sternly to be careful of what she said because I am a Virgo and I am certainly not critical, for heaven's sake. "I'm talking about pets," Ms. MacDonald said quickly. "Read my book. If you're a Virgo, you should select a Taurus pet. It's an earth sign, the same as you, and Taurians are one-man pets.

"If you're a fire sign, of course, you have to be careful about getting a water pet. It will just put out the fire."

I was beginning to get confused. "Taurus is an earth sign," she explained slowly. "And earth mixes with water. You must just be careful not to mix a fire owner with a water pet."

"What is the best sign for a pet?" I asked her a little desperately.

"Well," she said, "a Cancer is very fluid. That's a water sign, you know, but it will take on the shape of any vessel. It's an easygoing, adaptable, affectionate pet. A little emotional, though." She paused. "Of course, Pisces makes a nice little pet, too. They're a little shy. Gemini pets are good companions, but they're restless."

By now I was so confused I decided to make a chart.

IF YOU ARE	BEST PET	WORST PET
Aries	Leo	Cancer, Scorpio
Taurus	Taurus, Virgo, Capricorn	Gemini, Libra, Aquarius
Gemini	Gemini, Libra, Aquarius	Virgo
Cancer	Cancer, Scorpio, Pisces	Aries, Libra
Leo	Leo, Sagittarius	Aries
Virgo	Taurus	Cancer, Sagittarius
Libra	Libra, Gemini	Aries, Cancer
Scorpio	Scorpio, Capricorn	Cancer
Sagittarius	Sagittarius, Aries, Leo	Pisces, Cancer
Capricorn	Taurus	Aries, Leo, Virgo
Aquarius	Gemini, Aries, Sagittarius	Leo
Pisces	Cancer, Taurus	Virgo

There now. But promise me you won't ask me to believe it.

Q. *I've read stories of dogs traveling amazing distances to return to their homes. How far actually have they gone?* —P. Y., SAN ANGELO, TEX.

A. Take your pick. One dog went 750 miles—from Denver to Des Moines—and over snow-covered highways, too. His name was Max, and he was a German shepherd owned by Mr. and Mrs. Robert L. Martin. They had taken Max with them when they moved to Denver, but Max, on his own, moved back. More recently, there was a story from Italy about another German shepherd that made a similar journey from Brindisi to Milan—a distance of 745 miles. It took her four months. In *The Incredible Journey*, Sheila Burnford's great book about the old English bull terrier, the young Labrador retriever and the extraordinary Siamese cat, the distance covered was only 200 miles. But remember, the three animals kept together and had to face the perils of the wilds of northwest Ontario.

Finally, try this one. Once upon a time—actually the date was April 20, 1922—a terrier appeared at the Government Dock in Vancouver, British Columbia. He was immediately noticed by several crewmen and dockmen because of his strange actions. He would board a boat and go straight to the cargo and sniff around it. It didn't seem to satisfy him and he would shortly go and do the same thing on another boat. Finally, he boarded one ship which was loading pulp and paper. This time he did not leave—he stayed on board and stowed away. In fact, he was not discovered on board the ship until the next day when, far out at sea, he suddenly appeared outside the captain's door.

The captain tried to make friends with the dog. So did the crew. But the dog remained aloof. According to Captain Kenneth Dodson, who would later write the dog's story, "he allowed his head to be patted but showed no return of affection."

Finally, the coast of Honshu was sighted—and at this the dog became extremely interested, sniffing the land breeze with obvious anticipation. And, when the ship anchored near the customs jetty, the dog became incredibly alert. He maintained an eager watch of all nearby boats. Suddenly a Dutch ship appeared. The dog now reached a fever pitch of excitement, and as a small boat from that ship came close he started to bark wildly. This attracted the attention of one of the men in the little boat. Shading his eyes, he saw the dog—and now his excitement matched that of the dog. But before the little boat could pull alongside, the dog's excitement got the better of him, and he leaped into the water—only to be pulled out and, as you've probably guessed, reunited with his master.

The dog's name, it seems, was Hector. His owner, the second mate of the Dutch ship, had given him a last run on the dock before taking off from Vancouver, and Hector, for some reason— perhaps because he got himself into a confined area—arrived back at the ship too late. It had already sailed. But Hector was not too late to travel, by his own instinct and intelligence, some five thousand miles to find his master. And, until a better example of devotion comes along, this one will have to do.

Q. *You wrote of a dog that went 745 miles. Don't you know cats have gone much further than that?* —C. D. LITTLETON, N.H.

A. No, I didn't. But since you wrote, I've discovered that there is a documented case of a New York veterinarian who had to leave his cat in New York and took up a new job and a new house in California. Five months later the cat appeared and, according to Fernand Nery, calmly "entered the house, jumped onto the familiar armchair that had for so long been his 'interior territory,' installed itself there and fell asleep."

Q. *Is it true that human beings have poor hearing compared to other animals? I had thought our senses were superior.* —K. J., ALTON, ILL.

A. Far from it, I'm afraid, although people can hear better than some animals, and see better than some; but the truth is we don't rank high. Your own dog, just to take one random example from the animal kingdom, can hear sounds at two hundred yards that you couldn't pick up at twenty.

Q. *I've heard a lot about dolphins riding the bow waves of ships and guiding them through narrow passes. Do they really?* —M. G., DULUTH, MINN.

A. They do indeed—but not by riding bow waves. They do that for fun, and for a free ride. But there are many documented stories of dolphins guiding ships by swimming well ahead of them. The most remarkable of these stories was about a dolphin called Pelorus Jack, who for many years guided ships through French Pass, a channel through the D'Urville Islands off New Zealand. This channel is full of rocks and has extremely strong currents. It is so dangerous, in fact, that there have been hundreds of shipwrecks there. The dolphin first appeared in front of a schooner from Boston named the *Brindle*, when she was approaching the passage. The members of the crew, seeing the dolphin bobbing up and down in front of their ship, at first wanted to kill it—but the captain's wife talked them out of it. The dolphin then proceeded to guide the ship through the narrow channel. And for years after that he guided almost every ship that came through, in the same way. Then, years later, a drunken passenger on a ship named the *Penguin* took out a gun and shot at Pelorus Jack. He hit him, too, and Jack swam away. This time, though, the crew was furious and were all in favor of lynching the passenger. Pelorus Jack disappeared for two weeks. Then he reappeared, apparently recovered from his wound, and once again proceeded to guide ship after ship through the channel. Not, though, the *Penguin*. Indeed, when that ship showed up again, Jack immediately disappeared. Ironically, it was on a still later trip, unguided and going through French Pass, that the *Penguin* was wrecked, and a large number of passengers and crew were drowned.

Q. *Some time ago you wrote about the biggest elephant in the world, in Africa, I think. I heard he was killed by poachers. Is this true?* —S. B., SUN PRAIRIE, WIS.

A. Ahmed, the great elephant with the magnificent tusks, was not killed by poachers. He died of old age—heart failure—at the age of, or at least close to, seventy. Ahmed lived on Mount Marsabit ("the place of the bold") in Kenya. In the last years of his life he was protected by a special decree of Kenya's President Kenyatta, and toward the end of his life his bodyguard was increased from two to five men. And with good reason. Poachers in Kenya kill or maim an estimated one thousand elephants each month. And even Ahmed was found, after death, to have a bullet lodged in his right tusk. And remember—this is one of the best African countries for wildlife. Ahmed himself will, in a sense, live on—at least in the minds of those lucky enough ever to have seen him. But few got more than a glimpse: an eerie sight, as he moved slowly around his misty mountain, resting his tusks (ten feet long and weighing, together, 350 pounds) on the ground after every few steps.

One man wrote simply, "We were awestruck. What a privilege it was to be in the company of a king."

Q. *Who would you say was the greatest police dog that ever lived?*
—S. R., BAY VILLAGE, OHIO

A. The most famous were Strongheart and Rin Tin Tin. But if you mean an actual police dog, my nomination would have to go to Rex—or, as he was known, Rex of Scotland Yard.

Filmmaker Leo Handel, who himself owns an extraordinary police dog and has written a book about them, puts Rex ahead of all the others. In six years of service, from 1950 to 1956, Rex and his "person," Constable Arthur Holman, were credited with a total of 125 arrests for crimes ranging from petty theft to armed robbery and murder.

On one occasion, Rex leapt at a gunman and the latter shot him right in the face. Rex, blinded by powder burns, turned a backward somersault in midair and was knocked unconscious. But somehow the bullet missed his brain.

And even in that incredible case Constable Holman, saved by Rex's leap, got his man. Afterward, Rex recovered his eyesight and the dog, amazingly, continued working.

His most spectacular feat was the capture of a whole gang of gunmen, even though they all took off in different directions after shooting two of four constables. Rex got each man, one by one, knocked them over and stood guard over them until an unwounded constable arrived and the dog could move on to the next man. And remember, this was a dog who had once been shot right in the face.

Q. *I know you always talk about respect for all animal life, but I trust you do not include snails. Can you give me a single reason why I should allow them to devour my flower beds?* —I. M., WINNSBORO, TEX.

A. Of course I can. Snails are remarkable creatures. For one thing, they work their tails off all night so that you can wake up to a lawn shining with lacy silver trails. They can't help it that this makes them hungry for geraniums. For another thing, did you

know that twenty-five snails, properly harnessed, could pull a wagon with a 150-pound man in it. You need them in case your car breaks down. Finally, picture this—snails court one another. The male snail actually performs a ritual dance for the lady of his choice. Now can you, in all good conscience, go around stepping on these noble little beasts? Plant a special treat for them, I say.

Q. *I've heard about dolphins rescuing people. Are there any other wild animals known to aid people in distress?* —S. A., POTTSVILLE, PA.

A. Yes. The same behavior has been attributed to the misnamed "killer whales." West coast Indians, in particular, have many legends about riding to safety on the backs of these so-called monsters. Just last year another unusual aquatic samaritan was discovered—the giant sea turtle. A shipwreck victim in waters off Manila climbed aboard a passing turtle, which stayed at the surface and carried her for two full days until human rescuers appeared. Eyewitnesses thought the woman was floating on an oil drum until she was safely on board the boat—whereupon the "oil drum" circled the area twice and disappeared.

Q. *Our beagle, Toby, had a bad case of fleas and infected our mountain cabin last summer. We got rid of Toby's fleas, but on returning to the*

cabin this winter, we found the furniture still jumping with them. What's up? —R. L., DAWSON, GA.

A. Well, they're strange creatures, all right. For one thing, they always jump backward. Their most disconcerting quality— and we hate to tell you this—is that a population of them can live without eating for two years. Maybe you should plan to vacation at the coast until, say, 1979?

Q. *My cat seems to have periodic episodes of deafness. Usually he'll come right away when I call, but at other times I can practically yell at his back and he doesn't hear. What could cause this?* —P. M., MESA, ARIZ.

A. Unexplained episodes of deafness in cats are, in my experience, usually caused by something like you being away longer than the cat deems excusable. For example, it can be cured by explaining before you leave the house that you will indeed be back and by specifying when. You make, we believe, a grave error in thinking that your cat does not understand a word of English. Something you should be mindful of is how you speak of him to company. An indulgent little chuckle about how he is all bluff, or the revealing of some small secret of his, will not be lost on him and could cause a prolonged, serious deafness.

Cats will generally not chew the furniture or stoop to violence to show their displeasure with you—they are more likly to pretend you don't exist. They realize that to a cat person the emotional trauma of not being able to get a response is far worse than getting a scratch or finding the morning paper in shreds.

The next time you find yourself talking to his back and you think he can't hear have a look at his tail. If the tip of it is twitching abruptly back and forth, you'll know you have some fences to mend.

Q. *I have heard that birds sometimes warn animals that hunters are near. Is this true?* —M. J., DAINGERFIELD, TEX.

A. Yes. The so-called tick-birds, which live on the backs of antelopes, buffalo, zebras, warthogs and even elephants, often fly around and give warning to their "hosts" when hunters approach. The tick-bird is particularly helpful to the rhinoceros. According to zoologist Philip Street, the birds seem to know that the rhino has very poor eyesight and give louder and more frequent warnings for him than for any other animal.

Probably the most remarkable bird-animal association is the one between a bird called the spurr-winged lapwing and the crocodile. The lapwing goes right into the crocodile's mouth to pick off leeches. Not only is the bird not afraid of going into the crocodile's mouth but, for his part, the crocodile obviously knows the bird is helping him, because he never hurts it. Sometimes he closes his jaws, but he opens them again to let the bird out.

Q. *Some time ago you wrote about the racetrack which advertised "the world's fastest animal." I think you said the racehorse would be, among animals, sixth. Give us a list of speeds—man included.* —B. K., RED OAK, IOWA

A. Okay. *Natural History* magazine published the most complete list I've seen. Here it is:

ANIMALS	SPEEDS/MPH	ANIMALS	SPEEDS/MPH
cheetah	70	reindeer	32
pronghorn	61	giraffe	32
wildebeest	50	white-tailed deer	30
lion	50	warthog	30
Thomson's gazelle	50	grizzly bear	30
quarter horse	47.5	cat (domestic)	30
elk	45	man	27.89
cape hunting dog	45	elephant	25
coyote	43	black mamba snake	20
gray fox	42	six-lined race runner	18
hyena	40	squirrel	12
zebra	40	pig (domestic)	11
Mongolian wild ass	40	chicken	9
greyhound	39.35	spider	1.17
whippet	35.50	giant tortoise	0.17
rabbit (domestic)	35	three-toed sloth	0.15
mule deer	35	garden snail	0.03
jackal	35		

I've got some quarrels with this list. Although the magazine admits the maximum speeds were for approximately a quarter of a mile (hence the quarter horse instead of the racehorse), the lion and the elephant were clocked in the act of charging, which is somewhat different. Also, they obviously used the fastest man versus an average animal. The most remarkable thing about a cheetah's speed, incidentally, is its ability to accelerate—it can go from a standing stop to 45 m.p.h. in two seconds. Not even the fastest racing car can match this. Finally, I have never heard of a six-lined race runner. But then—probably he's never heard of me.

Q. *Who would have won in a race between Man O'War and Secretariat?* —C. M., LEBANON, OREG.

A. Man O' War. He was the greatest racehorse who ever lived. And he would have won in a walk, too, unless one thing happened: if in that particular race, I bet on him.

Q. *Have monkeys ever been used as jockeys?* —W. W., MEDFIELD, MAINE

A. Yes. Not on horses, though—on dogs. On the authority of Jimmy McGee, *San Francisco Examiner* sportswriter, I am informed that back in the 30s the owner of a stable of greyhounds also owned some monkeys and, at the Baden track in south San Francisco, he tried them out in actual races. All I can add is that greyhound racing is cruel enough, starting with the fact that they train the dogs with live rabbits, without adding a freak show. Maybe the owners of these tracks could race each other—and let the animals bet.

Q. *Is it true that chimpanzees can paint? I mean, seriously paint. Do people buy their paintings?* —H. B., CHAPPAQUA, N.Y.

A. Yes to both questions. And not just chimpanzees, either, but also orangutans, gorillas and capuchin monkeys. As a matter of fact, there is, if you can bear it, among the capuchins, an artist who goes by the name of Pablo—no relation, however. Betsy, a chimpanzee at the Baltimore zoo, is probably the most commercial of the chimp artists. Indeed, advertised as a "master" (there is, apparently, no Chimp Lib), she sold sixty-five paintings, one of them

for seventy-five dollars. The honor of being the most prolific of all chimp artists, however, must go to Congo of the London zoo. He finished over four hundred paintings. But where Congo was concerned, "finished" was a rather definite word. It seems that when urged to go on with the paintings he considered finished, he merely drew lines in all directions—in effect, crossing out his painting. People soon got the hint. And from then on, when Congo said a painting was finished, it was finished.

Usually you ask the questions and we give the answers. The following letter, however, asks and answers—and we couldn't resist it. We consider it our Letter of the Year.

The writer, B. Rule Stout, was for fifty-one years general manager of the Coal Creek Mining and Manufacturing Company in Knoxville, Tennessee. "On my ninety-fifth birthday," he writes, "I taught a Sunday school class, also filled a pulpit." Judging from his letter, we believe him!

Dear Bro Animal Lover,

Which is the most affectionate of all animals? I do not know, but I am nominating the common mountain groundhog or woodchuck, and here's why.

Back about 1920 I was running a longline between Andrew Braden and our company. Old Rusty, his hound, came along. That evening, when we were nearing the final corner, Old Rusty started baying at something very near the end of the line. We completed the end of the survey, then stepped down the mountain about fifty feet and found Rusty standing over a groundhog he had just killed. Also there were two very little groundpigs he had killed.

Andrew, running his hand back in the den, found a third, not hurt. I dropped it in my pocket, and drove the forty-four miles home, then handed it to my wife. It was about as long as a ground squirrel, but much heavier, weight perhaps a quarter of a pound. We got some milk in a spoon and it went for it, so we filled it up. It was about a week old. My wife named it Sausage.

I fixed it up a nice nest in a box, but in a week it was running all over the house, which it continued to do as long as it lived. But here's another thing. It was born housebroke, and never once did it leave any kind of mess. When it wanted to go out in the yard, it would come pull your pants or dress, chatter, then run to the door. Soon there had to be an understanding between Sausage and our dog, Moses, and when Moses picked up a slice of stale bread, Sausage nipped her on the front leg, and after that, Moses let Sausage have what she liked, mostly just bread. The neighbors had dogs, and they soon learned she was a pet, and, like Moses, gave her the right of way.

When grown, Sausage weighed thirteen pounds, but as she grew up and as long as she lived, she would meet me, much like a shepherd dog, but chattering, then run upon my shoulder and chatter for a couple of minutes. Could I have understood her language I know she was telling me how much she loved me. But she was even more affectionate to my wife, and often I would see her up on Mrs. Stout's shoulder, talking as hard as she could.

But one night she was gone, and for three weeks we never heard of her. Then our laundryman said, "Have you lost your groundhog? If so, I know where it is." And he told us. My wife hitched the horse to the buggy and drove to the address, went in, asked and was told, "Yes, we have a groundhog out there in that barrel. It is the meanest thing I ever saw and will eat you up." Mrs. Stout said, "Take off the cover, we have a pet that is gone and I want to see if it is ours."

Again the lady said, "Don't dare stick your hand in that barrel or it will bite it off." My wife said, "If it is Sausage, it won't bite me," so as the top came off my wife said, "Yo Sausage," and started sticking her hand down, but she got no further, as Sausage ran right up her shoulder and started chattering her little heart out.

Some months later, again she disappeared and forever. But the family never had a pet we loved more or that loved us more or that could show its affection so well.

— B. RULE STOUT

Q. *You wrote about a coyote who managed to get along on two legs, one front and one back. I don't believe it.* —B. W., MESA, TEX.

A. Will you accept a dog? His name is Scotty, he's owned by a doctor and his wife and their four children, and he lives in New Zealand. He's six years old. Four years ago he was hit by an automobile and had to have his left hind leg removed at the hip joint and his left front leg removed at the shoulder joint. His family were not only determined to save him, they were determined to make him mobile. At first, to help him learn balance, they took a towel and held it taut under his stomach. In a short time he was moving without any towel, and today he goes about like any other dog. He jumps, he runs up and down flights of steps and he can even keep up with a cantering horse. Although he is fed sparingly—to keep him from gaining too much weight—he is full of energy and the joy of living. The only thing he can't do by himself is stand still. When he wants to do that, he uses a wall, a chair, or the leg of one of his family.

Q. *What is the most remarkable achievement you know of made by a dog?* —W. E., MALVERN, N. Y.

A. Well, until a more remarkable one comes along, a man I know in Tarzana, California, named Ken Smith taught his dog to fly. She's a German shepherd, and Mr. Smith first took her flying with him when she was six weeks old. He built her a special harness and, now sixteen years old, she still flies regularly with him and has logged over three hundred flying hours.

The plane has dual controls, and when she sees one wing go down, she yelps, turns the wheel and makes the wing go up until it is again even with the other wing. I asked Mr. Smith how his dog handles communications with the tower. "Perfectly," he answered. "Her name is Radar."

Q. *Some time ago you wrote that cats like to swim. I disagree. My cat won't go near the water.* —L. A., CARMEL, CALIF.

A. I don't say all cats like to swim—just some cats. Recently I was in Las Vegas watching two cats swimming in a pool. And don't say the Las Vegas sun addled their brains; they were obviously loving it. They are owned by a former New York model named Marti Scholl, who has a television show out there. She has an eight-month-old male cat named Tony and a three-month-old female named Samantha. Both were strays.

Some time ago, when it was one hundred degrees in the shade and they were panting, she got into her pool, taking one cat under each arm, and then very gradually, little by little, dunked them until they actually pulled away and started swimming.

The cats still don't get into the pool by themselves, Ms. Scholl reports, but on days she feels are too cool for them to go swimming, they'll often sit by the side of the pool and meow to get in. They often swim the whole length of the pool, down and back, and can get out by themselves.

Ms. Scholl lives near the golf course and has lately noticed the cats taking long looks at the golfers. She is, however, not considering outfitting them with clubs.

Q. *Did you hear about the otter who went into the bank in England?* —P. T., SNOHOMISH, WASH.

A. Indeed I did. And your four-legged friend at Great Britain's Clydesdale Bank received a warm welcome. He entered the bank on its so-called Open House Day. He did not, however, open an account, cash a check or make a deposit. Instead, after a brief wait in line, he marched solemnly upstairs, shortly to be trailed by a search party led by the hastily summoned local veterinarian. But by this time the otter was playing hide-and-seek, and the search failed. Then, the next morning, lo and behold, the otter reappeared and marched solemnly down the stairs and out into the street.

Q. *When I went out West I was told that a cow's identification of her calf is so infallible that even courts of law take it over other evidence. Is this true?* —M. O., MISSOURI VALLEY, IOWA

A. It is indeed. In his book, *Roundup at Double Diamond—The American Cowboy Today*, author Bill Surface cites a case in Wise County, Texas, in which a rustler was apprehended entirely on the basis of a cow sniffing her calf out from every calf in the pasture. The Wise sheriff himself provided the bottom line. "This," he said, "is better than fingerprints."

Q. *What can you tell me about Bertha, the famous trained elephant at the casino in Sparks, Nevada?* —F. J., COLUMBIA, MO.

A. One thing I can tell you is that keeping a ten-thousand-pound elephant in a casino (it's at a place called The Nugget) is something I don't approve of. However, Bertha is really an extraordinary animal. According to Jenda Smaha, an extraordinary elephant handler who worked with Bertha for years, she is the Einstein of the elephant world. Crazy about Smaha, too. She used to wake him up from his preshow nap by brushing her eyelashes against his cheek. Picture that!

Bertha definitely has a sense of humor. Witness this story. Smaha used to keep all of his performing paraphernalia—including Bertha's sugar treats—in a locked cabinet in Bertha's "elephant house." Although it would have been a snap to break the cabinet and raid the goodies, Bertha knew it was taboo. Yet she wasn't above using devious strategy to satisfy her sweet tooth.

She would lie in wait for some stranger to happen into the elephant house (it had to be someone who didn't know she was five tons of pure marshmallow), then startle the guest by grabbing an arm with her trunk. If the visitor tried to pull away, the grip would tighten menacingly.

Thus cowed, the visitor would be led to the cabinet, where his hand would be placed on the handle. Seeing the lock, it would dawn on the visitor that he or she was being pressed into complicity as a criminal. The decision of which would be more dangerous—enraging Bertha or braving the wrath of the fierce Smaha—had to be difficult.

One young woman, however, figured on getting out of it by protesting to Bertha that the cabinet was padlocked. She thought she had succeeded when Bertha let go of her arm, but as she made for the exit there was a tap on her shoulder. Turning around, she found herself once again face to face with the trunk, but this time it was holding—what else—the key.

The woman gave up. She married Smaha.

Q. *Cats have lived after falling from incredible heights. How?*
—R. P., SORO, MO.

A. I don't know how, and I wouldn't tell you if I did. This ability is an old wives' tale, is vastly exaggerated and is the reason for such vicious cruelty as children dropping cats off roofs. Actually, I know of one cat who broke all four legs and several teeth from a fall of just one story.

Q. *You're always writing about dog heroics. How about the times cats have saved people?* —W. G., ELMORE, ALA.

There are literally hundreds of such stories. A Washington, D.C., cat leaped on the bed of the head of its family during a household fire and scratched him in the face until he woke. The cat was credited with saving the lives of six people. In Oconto, Wisconsin, Pat, a twenty-pound cat, heard two burglars downstairs, ran into her mistress's room and not only woke the mistress but made such a racket the burglars left. In Battle Creek, Michigan, a man entered the house of an elderly woman on the pretext of being a meter-reader and hurled the woman to the floor. At that moment, the woman's cat leaped from the mantle and raked the intruder's neck with her claws. The man not only relaxed his hold on the woman; he ran for his life.

And now a word for "watch cats," like one named Emily Hogan, who one day called her household's attention to the window where she was sitting by growling repeatedly. When they went over to the window and looked out in the direction Emily was looking—across the way—there was a man climbing into a neighbor's apartment window. The police were called and found that, indeed, a criminal had broken into the place, and if not for Emily, the neighbor would have been in great danger. Apparently, none of the dogs in the neighborhood raised so much as a woof. Emily, who is small, stoutish, gray and white and occasionally bad-tempered, is the heroine of East Tenth Street.

Q. *You wrote not long ago about cats being smarter than dogs. Well, you've never heard of a Seeing Eye cat, have you?* —A. S., GARDEN GROVE, CALIF.

A. Loathe as we are to lose your friendship—yes, we have. Her name is Rhubarb, and she's ten years old. For nine and a half of those years she has served as the eyes of her totally blind mistress, Elsa Schneider of San Diego. "I could have had a Seeing Eye dog," says Mrs. Schneider, "but I got Rhubarb first, and I couldn't handle a dog, too. I thought, 'Well, as long as I have her, let's see what we can do.' It took me about six months to start leash training. At first she was like a little bay steer jumping up and down, but after about two weeks she had adjusted to it." Now, according to Mrs. Schneider, Rhubarb takes great pride in her responsibilities, leading Mrs. Schneider flawlessly through the house, down the stairs and to and from their various daily destinations. She's a guard cat, too. "The telephone man won't come in unless I put her in the bedroom," says Mrs. Schneider. "She lays her little ears back, opens her mouth and hisses—then she growls, just like a dog."

Rhubarb fetches, too—but only Mrs. Schneider. "If I'm outside and she hears the phone, she gives me a yell and runs for the back door to bring me to the house," Mrs. Schneider says, "then she hurries across the dining room to the phone. If she thinks I've been talking too long, she puts her paws on my legs and gives me a yell." Rhubarb does not consider herself an ordinary house cat, either. "She's not a real pet cat," Mrs. Schneider says, "she's all business. But lots of times she'll let me pick her up and I wrap her in a blanket and I rock her like a baby. And she'll go to sleep. She loves that blanket best of all."

Q. *You're always writing about dogs and cats who do heroic things. How about birds? Aren't they smart enough?* —G. R., DECATUR, ILL.

A. Never underestimate the intelligence of a bird. Will you settle for a heroic canary? Once upon a time—actually the time was 1950—a canary named Bibs lived in Hermitage, Tennessee, with an elderly woman whom everyone called Aunt Tess. The only other occupant of the house was a cat. It seems Aunt Tess's niece thought her aunt too old to live alone and was constantly worried about her. The niece and her husband lived within sight of Aunt Tess's house, and each night, before drawing the curtains, made a habit of being sure Aunt Tess's lights were on, which indicated that everything was all right over there. However, one night, after she had done this, the niece heard a tapping on the window, and even heard what she afterward said sounded like a loud cry. She went to the window, drew the curtains back and there was Bibs, tapping and beating against the glass. And, literally as she was watching, Bibs dropped dead from exhaustion on the sill. Immediately the niece knew something was wrong and she and her husband ran over to Aunt Tess's house. They found her unconscious and bleeding after a bad fall. Bibs had saved her life.

Q. *You wrote about a long-haired dachshund from Portland, Oregon, who liked to ski. How do you know?* —L. G., KULPSVILLE, PA.

A. I asked him. No, seriously, I had many letters about the skiing dog, Schmaltz, including one from his owner, Dr. Clagett Harding.

He wears four little ski boots—front and back on one ski and front and back on the other—and can, with ears and tail kind of winging and ruddering, and with seeming enjoyment, go down remarkably steep slopes. The only thing Schmaltz can't do is stop. And I know what you're going to say to that. The fact is, though, if Dr. Harding is at the top of the slope, he always sees to it that Schmaltz has a catcher at the bottom. Schmaltz also, incidentally, skates. He does not, however, play basketball.

Dr. Harding told me, among other things, that Schmaltz can walk with skis on level terrain and can even, "if snow, weather and spirit is right," jump. He also told me that his four boots—two for each ski—are made from plaster casts of his feet and that, if they are put on the wrong foot, Schmaltz chews on the doctor's hand

and then he corrects them. The doctor says he has four reasons for believing that Schmaltz really enjoys skiing: "(1) most animals love motion without effort, (2) the faster we ski, the faster his tail wags, (3) if snow is wet or slushy, he will lie down and won't ski and (4) whenever a member of the family picks up skis, Schmaltz will run to his closet and drag out his equipment."

Q. *You wrote about great animal books, but you never mentioned my favorite of all,* Beautiful Joe —P. D., SAN DIEGO, CALIF.

A. It was an unpardonable omission. As *Black Beauty* remains the classic book of the horse, so *Beautiful Joe* remains the classic book of the dog. It first appeared in 1892 and was written by Marshall Saunders, a woman. One of Canada's best-loved writers of children's books, she wrote *Beautiful Joe* in the first-person style, as a supposed autobiography.

Joe was not beautiful, of course; he was the opposite of beautiful. Born a mutt, he was cruelly treated by a terrible owner, who not only killed his mother's other puppies, and also his mother, but who also took a hatchet and cut off Joe's ears and tail as close to his body as he could.

The story sounds too awful to be true, but, sadly, it *was* true—it was based on the life of a real dog in Meaford, Ontario. The amazing thing about *Beautiful Joe* is that it is very long for a children's book—256 packed pages—and though Joe's life is happy after the first awful part, it goes into every kind of cruelty to other animals, from rabbits to circus animals.

Nonetheless, the book, currently published by McClelland and Stewart, Ltd., in Toronto, has been one of the most successful children's books of all time. To this day, there is a monument and a whole park in Meaford devoted to the memory of Beautiful Joe.

Q. *Paul Gallico once wrote a short poem about man from a cat's point of view. I saw it in a friend's library, but I've never been able to run it down since. Do you know the one I mean?* —S. A., ALTURAS, CALIF.

A. It's in the late Mr. Gallico's book, *Honourable Cat*, and it's called "Man." I love it as much as you do, and here it is.

> Long-nosed. nose.
> Silly clothes.
> No paws.
> Useless claws.
> Harsh cry.
> False eye.
> Talk, talk.
> Monkey walk.
> No fur.
> No purr.
> Face pale.
> No tail.
> Rotten planners.
> No manners.
> Big bragger.
> Just swagger.
> Lives in cell.
> Bad smell.
> Self admire.
> Big liar.
> Unjust.
> Can't trust.
> Friend untrue.
> Man, that's You.

Q. *Who would you say was the most famous dog who ever lived?*
—R. S., WILLITS, CALIF.

A. My nomination would have to go to a dog who never had a home of his own; who, for fifteen years of his life, never had an owner; and who, for the very short time that he did have one, was disowned by that owner. Nonetheless, he is so famous that although he died over a hundred years ago countless books and stories and even a movie have been made about him, and people still flock to his grave—one which stands, together with a monument to him, in a churchyard in Edinburgh. His name was Greyfriars Bobby. But even this came to him only after his death. In life he was just plain Bobby. He was a wee Skye terrier who as a puppy attached himself to an elderly Edinburgh shepherd named Auld Jock. (The court physician of Queen Elizabeth I once described a Skye as "a Cur which by reason of the length of heare makes showe neither a face nor body.") But if the little terrier from the famous island of Skye showed neither face nor body, courage and loyalty he did show. And when Auld Jock, dying, took a copper from his pocket to pay a restaurant owner for Bobby's meal and declared, "Bobby isn'a ma ain dog," Bobby, at least, never believed him. Jock died in 1858 and Bobby was not only the only mourner to follow him to his grave but afterward, first ordered away and then kicked at by the gravediggers, bravely stood his ground. And from then on, for fourteen years, day and night, he stayed on, save for one brief trip each day to that same restaurant for a bun, which he would solemnly carry back and eat near the grave. The first winter he took shelter under a nearby tombstone. By the next, the citizens of Edinburgh had erected a shelter for him. Finally, fourteen years later, he was buried beside his master.

Animals and
Their Famous
Friends

Q. *What kind of a cat is Jacqueline Onassis supposed to look like?*
—N. E., FALMOUTH, MASS.

A. A hep cat? No, I'm kidding. She is supposed to look like a Siamese cat. There was a famous party once where everyone came as his or her favorite animal. Most of the women came as some kind of wildcat and most of the men came, of course, as wolves or gorillas, or even as goats. My favorite, though, was the young boy who came as a male chauvinist piglet.

Q. *I see Jacqueline Onassis's so-called great fall look includes an Yves St. Laurent fox-trimmed sweater. What's the matter with her?* —V. P., L'ANSE, MICH.

A. What would you expect of a fox-hunter married to a whaler? Seriously, ever since Mrs. Onassis made the mistake of accepting that leopard coat years ago, her record on furs has not been too bad. She's at least gotten part of the message—no endangered furs—if not the whole message—no wild furs.

Mr. Onassis was, indeed, a whaler—with a vengeance. He started his whaling fleet in the late 1940s, and it was probably the most modernized one ever, complete with ten "units," a "mother ship," sixteen "chasers" and two tankers, not to mention a helicopter, radar equipment and explosive harpoons. This murderous flotilla, which cost sixty thousand dollars a day to operate, was apparently under orders to harpoon every whale it sighted. And, in so doing, it ran afoul not just of outraged humanitarians but of entire nations.

At one time the Peruvian navy, feeling Mr. Onassis's fleet had violated Peru's offshore limits, attacked the flagship and seized the fleet. At another time, the Norwegian government tied up a shipload of his whale oil. The Norwegians, according to George Carpozi, charged Onassis with exceeding whale quotas, catching whales out of season and violating limitations on their minimum size. Onassis settled by paying $435,000 to the Norwegian whaling industry and then finally sold his fleet in 1956 to the Japanese for $8,500,000. The bar stools on Mr. Onassis's famous yact *Christina* were covered, he once told me proudly, with the skins of whales' private parts. I'm glad to say I wasn't the only one on board who was disgusted—and who didn't sit at the bar.

Q. *Is it true that Charles Lindbergh is buried with animals?* —H. K., AVON PARK, FLA.

A. I visited Lindbergh's grave on the beautiful Hawaiian island of Maui. The grave is in a tiny churchyard, where three gibbons are also buried. When he was choosing his grave site, Lindbergh heard criticism about the fact that he had chosen a place where animals are buried. So he went to his friend Samuel Pryor, whose pet gibbons had long been friends of Lindbergh's, and asked specifically if he could have the grave next to them. The only writing on the tombstone says: "Charles A. Lindbergh—born, Michigan, 1902, Died, Maui, 1974."

Q. *Is it true that John Wayne was nicknamed for a dog?* —S. H., TROY, PA.

A. Yes, it is. As a child Mr. Wayne used to walk his dog

named Duke, and when people heard him call his dog, they started calling him—well, after the dog. As for some of Mr. Wayne's recent pictures, people have also been known to call them not after dogs but rather—just dogs. Incidentally, I don't approve of this, either. It's an anti-animal expression.

Q. *Where did Doris Day get her feeling for animals?* —S. W., DAWS, TEX.

A. Doris told me she got it from her mother—but she does not believe love of animals is inherited. "I don't think things really are inherited," she said. "I think we are individuals and we are all on our own." Doris also told me a story she didn't know whether I would dare print or not. "It was when I was very young," she said, "and we were living in Cincinnati and the people next door had a big, young dog outside in the yard. I loved him very much and then they went away for a whole long weekend and left him in the very cold weather. They left the dog to fend for himself without water or food. I never forgot it and I never spoke to them again. The dog cried and we took him in. And then, before they got back, we took him away to my uncle's house, and never said a word about it. He had the greatest life, that dog—the greatest!"

Q. *I hear Glenn Ford thinks all animals are great. What does he think is the greatest?* —B. F., DUBUQUE, IOWA

A. I put the question to Glenn, and he had no difficulty with his answer. "Dolphins," he said. "I like all animals but dolphins are the greatest. Remember, I was in the Navy and I really got to know dolphins." Glenn paused. "Cleveland," he went on earnestly, "I think that anyone who mistreats a dolphin should get exactly the same penalty as anyone who mistreats a human being. For murdering dolphins, I believe in capital punishment."

Q. *Is it true that Susan Saint James had a clause in her TV series contract that said that she didn't have to wear a fur coat on her program?* —A. C., NEW ORLEANS, LA.

A. No, the actual wording was much stronger than that. Susan and her husband, Tom Lucas, are both long-time members on the board of The Fund for Animals, and there is no subject on which they feel more strongly than the wearing of wild fur—i.e., leghold-trapped—coats. When Susan's contract as the co-star of "MacMillan and Wife" was being renegotiated at NBC, she and Tommy inserted a clause that states that if, at any time, in any scene, a wild fur coat was brought on the set, Susan was permitted to go home. Needless to say, and given the logistics of shooting a series in which Susan appeared in almost every scene, this meant no fur coats on "MacMillan and Wife."

Q. *Is Cindy Williams, of "Laverne and Shirley" fame, a real animal person?* —J. M., CRAFTON, PA.

A. She sure is. In fact, there are few people more dedicated to helping animals in all of Hollywood—she's even making a movie with her own money about an animal. It's called *Nigel Fox*, and it's about a fox hunt. "Nigel," she told us, "thinks people are real nice to him when they catch him and feed him. And then, the next day, of course, they let him go just to hunt him. I have a terrific ending."

Ms. Williams grew up in Texas, where her father raised pigs. "We had all kinds of animals," she told us, "stray cats, dogs, anything that moved. My mother has worked all her life as a waitress—she was a waitress then and she's still a waitress—and I remember her saying, 'Cindy, if you bring one more animal into this house. . . .' She didn't mean it, of course. In fact, she's got all my animals now—four cats and two dogs—because she's got a yard. My father pretended to be just as tough, but he wasn't at all. I remember one day there was a litter of pigs, and one little runt that the mother wouldn't feed. My father kept the little one in the oven and tried to save him for the longest time. But, eventually, he died."

"My movie," she said firmly, "is going to have a *happy* ending."

Q. *Zsa Zsa Gabor is always talking about her love of animals. What kind of dogs or cats has she?* —F. W., REDDING, CALIF.

A. Zsa Zsa has three Shih Tzus and one kuvasz. The latter, the Hungarian kings' dog, is snow white. The three Shih Tzus are black and white. Their names are Genghis, Sugar and Sammy Davis, Jr. "Ze Shih Tzus, dollink," she told me, "iz ze Tibetan temple dog. In ze whole world zair is no dog like it. Centuries ago, ze empress of China mixed a Lhasa apso vis her Pekingese, and zat became the Shih Tzu. Zey are very intelligent. Genghis is terribly intelligent. I never had a husband half as intelligent."

I thought I understood Zsa Zsa to say that J. Paul Getty has given her a Shih Tzu. "No, no, dollink," she corrected. "I gave a Shih Tzu to J. Paul Getty. J. Paul Getty never gave anybody anyzing."

Q. *Please settle an argument. I say Joe Namath was the first male celebrity to wear a fur coat. My boyfriend says it was Liberace.* —W. F., BIDDEFORD, MAINE

A. Your boyfriend wins. Liberace was first—with, of all cruel coats, a white beaver. The irony is that I'll bet Liberace was told it was ranched. Beavers are not ranched anywhere; they are trapped.

Q. *Is Princess Grace really into animals?* —C. B., WORTHINGTON, CONN.

A. Her Serene Highness, the Princess of Monaco, is "into" them indeed. In fact, in my capacity as president of the Fund for Animals, I had the honor of announcing the princess as the new international chairman of the Fund for Animals. The princess feels particularly strongly on the subject of fur. "I cannot stand," she said, "the idea that wild animals can be killed to satisfy fashion."

I asked her if this feeling began early in her life. "Very early," she told me. "As children, we always had animals around—dogs, cats, canaries, everything. My brother even had an alligator."

Her family today feels the same way. Prince Rainier, for example, has an extraordinary personal relationship with the animals in Monaco's zoo. On my desk is a picture he gave me of a chimpanzee hugging him—and him hugging back. As for Princesses Caroline and Stephanie, they took petitions around Monaco and even raised money to stop the killing of baby seals. They also went directly to shopkeepers to try to get them to stop selling seal coats.

Princess Grace, incidentally, sees no division between her animal cause and her many "people" causes, such as the Red Cross. "I think they're the same thing," she told me. "It's a feeling for life—all life."

Q. *What kind of animals has Dick Van Dyke owned?* —J. N., GRANT TOWN, W. VA.

A. "What I've fed," Mr. Van Dyke told me, "and what I've owned are two different things. I fed a pack of coyotes every day for months. I got up to the third generation of them. They came right up to my front porch in Arizona every night. You can't con them, though, and they wouldn't come too close. And if I hadn't put the food and water down by a certain time, they'd just sit and howl." What, we asked, about his dogs? Mr. Van Dyke smiled.

"During coyote feeding time," he said, "the dogs barked very fero-ciously—but only from inside the house. Even my Great Dane, Nelson, is actually scared to death of coyotes."

Q. *I have heard that Gloria Swanson has had just about every kind of pet in her life. What kind does she think makes the best pet?* —D. P., DENTON, TEX.

A. I put the question to Ms. Swanson out in Hollywood, by asking her to begin at the beginning—which, with her, isn't yester-day. She couldn't remember all of her pets, but the first one she ever had was a black cat.

She was a very young girl, and she used to put a doll's bonnet on it and take it around in a doll's pram. Today she's not proud of that, and thinks children should never be allowed to make dolls out of pets.

Ms. Swanson's next pet, when she was still very young and lived on an Army post in Key West, was an alligator. "At least," she told me, "I didn't take that around in a pram."

When she first went to Hollywood, she was, she said, at the "horse-crazy stage." However, when she first started in pictures—she starred almost right away—she was still going riding regularly in the Hollywood hills.

On one of her birthdays, she remembers, she was given a crop as a present by Rudolph Valentino. This year, no less than three movies are being made about Valentino—he's the biggest nostalgia item on today's Hollywood menu—but Ms. Swanson remembers him, at the time he gave her the crop, as a man who was not only not a star but just an extra. "But he was pushing very hard," she said, "and he sure was dreaming about being a star."

Once, in London, at the height of Ms. Swanson's world fame, she looked down from her hotel window in Piccadilly and saw some kind of strange animal riding in the back seat of a car. "From up there," she told me, "it looked just like a lot of feathers blowing. I had to have one, whatever it was."

So the next day, sailing back on one of the Queens, sure enough, Miss Swanson had on board with her an Olde English sheepdog.

Taking the dog to her home at Croton-on-Hudson presented a problem. She already had chows, and the chows were mean to the intruder and sheep-killers as well.

The most incredible thing they did was to teach the Olde English sheepdog to bring home bones in his mouth. So he was the one who got blamed.

"Chows," Ms. Swanson says, "are very devious dogs."

To get to your question at long last, Ms. Swanson's favorite: She thought a long time and said, "I think it would be a dachshund. I remember my Max so well. They can be so stubborn. They're basically Germanic, you know. They're so clean. My Max was almost as clean as my first love—my black cat."

Q. *I saw you on "The Dinah Shore Show." Dinah seems to care very much about animals. What kind of animals does she have, and what kind was she brought up on?* —M. W., MANVILLE, N.J.

A. I asked Ms. Shore your question, and she told me that

when she was a little girl she had cats, a dog, turtles, fish and birds. But she also told me frankly that her mother and father were not, as she puts it, "all that crazy about animals"—that, in fact, her father would never allow her to have a big dog.

"It was like he wouldn't let me have a big bike," Ms. Shore told me. "He was afraid either one would hurt me."

To this day she would like nothing better than a really big dog—"the bigger the better." Right now, though, she's more satisfied with a large female basset named Grunk. "Grunk was recently married," Ms. Shore told me, "and we now have eight beautiful bassetnets."

I told her sternly I disapproved—Grunk should have been spayed. But Ms. Shore promised she already had homes for every single one of the pups—if, she added, "I can bear to part with any of them."

Interestingly enough, Ms. Shore also still has turtles and fish. "The only thing I miss that I had as a child is a cat. But my Pauline (Ms. Shore's extraordinary housekeeper) is frightened of them. Someone threw one in her face when she was a little girl and she never got over it."

Nonetheless, both Ms. Shore and Pauline together help feed the neighborhood's stray cats.

Q. *You say Charo is a great animal lover. Give me an example.*
—D. R., BOSTON, MASS.

A. Will you accept that she's an international smuggler of animals? Seriously, on a trip to Japan when she found she couldn't take her Chihuahua, Delilah, across the border she got her sister, Carmen, to wear Delilah—under a large blouse. The only trouble was that when their mother, back in Spain, saw their picture in the paper, she was very upset. She cabled Charo and Carmen to come home immediately, that she was heartbroken that her unmarried daughter would appear in public, as she put it, "in that condition." Charo's mother is still, incidentally, not entirely sold on the Delilah story.

Q. *Hugh O'Brian looks like an animal man. Is he?* —G. C., FT. COLLINS, COLO.

A. Mr. O'Brian and I don't agree about hunting, but he is very much a dog man—in fact, he told me he'd never in his life been without "being owned" by one. At present, in his Beverly Hills home, he has two. One is a white German shepherd named Brut. "He gets into my Faberge," Mr. O' smiles, "all the time." Then he added, seriously, "You know, up until a few years ago, they used to kill all the white ones. How stupid. Now they have them registered. Brut is my third generation of whites." Mr. O'Brian admitted, however, that the real ruler of his house was not the hundred-pound Brut, but a small fifteen-pound female mutt named Panda. "She looks like a panda, too. Her father was a chihuahua and her mother was half a toy collie and half about a dozen other breeds. Don't ask me how it happened." "How," we asked, "did it happen?" "Love," he said, "can climb mountains."

Q. *I would like to know if Helen Hayes loves animals. She looks as if she does.* —A. G., BISMARCK, N. DAK.

A. Ms. Hayes does, indeed. She told me she now has "only" two poodles—she got them in Mexico—but in the course of her life she's had as many as eleven pets at one time. Her favorite of all, she said, was a pet squirrel. It was named Freddie and she and her husband, the late Charles MacArthur, reared it from injured babyhood to full-grown boss of the household.

"He loved to terrorize guests," Ms. Hayes said, "by dropping from the ceiling onto their heads. But once in a while he played tricks on us, too. Sometimes in the middle of the night I'd hear Charlie utter a terrifying scream. But I knew it wasn't a nightmare. All that had happened was that Freddie had gotten cold and had gotten into bed with him."

Q. *I know Hugh Downs is into ecology in a big way. Is he also an animal person?* —M. M., GRASS VALLEY, CALIF.

A. Hugh told me he grew up on a farm in Ohio and always had both dogs and cats. He's now living in Carefree, Arizona. "Right in town," he smiles, "but remember, the town's population is 400." He, like his friend, Dick Van Dyke, is a real coyote person. "The ranchers exaggerate their depredations incredibly," he told me. "Coyotes are wonderful animals." Hugh and his wife, Ruth, regularly take their garbage to a dump where they stand and watch the coyotes feed. "They stand and look at us, too," Hugh says, "and they're also pretty critical of what's on the menu. But there's only one thing they won't eat at all—cauliflower. Spinach, even broccoli, is okay, but not cauliflower."

Q. *Who would win in a race between Mark Spitz and a seal?* —S. P., PASCO, WASH.

A. No contest. A California sea lion has been clocked at 25 miles an hour. Spitz, setting the world's record for 100 meters, averaged a mere 4.31 miles an hour. In a down-and-back pool race, the seal would be finished by the time Spitz got one-third of the way down. Our guess is the seal could also do a more convincing commercial. At least he'd get it over quicker.

Q. *Does Joey Bishop like animals?* —R. J., WACO, TEX.

A. Indeed he does. Joey is not only a dog man, he is an underdog man, and told me he would never forget the first dog he ever had, a fox terrier. "We grew up together," he said, "in south Philadelphia." Joey and his wife, who is also an animal lover, now have a four-year-old Yorkshire, but their favorite dog was a farm collie that Buddy Hacket was responsible for. "I said to Buddy," Joey recalls, " 'go to a pet shop and get me a small, healthy, male dog that doesn't shed.' So what did Buddy do? He went not to a pet shop but to the shelter and got me not a small male dog that didn't shed but a great big friendly female who shed all the time. And then he wouldn't even take responsibility for it. 'Your son,' Buddy said, 'picked it out.' But you know what?" Joey concludes. "She was the very best dog I ever had."

Q. *I know Bing Crosby is an avid hunter. Is it true that even his daughter hunts?* —N. H., FAIRMOUNT, IND.

A. It's true, all right. On a safari in east Kenya, fifteen-year-old Mary Frances Crosby shot, right between the eyes, a crocodile. "I'm getting the skin for a pair of shoes and a pocketbook," she was quoted as saying, smiling. Incredibly enough, she has already bagged—you will excuse the expression—one Ecologist-of-the-Month Award. Herewith another. Not smiling, though; crying. With crocodile tears, of course.

Q. *Is it true that Gardner McKay was bitten by one of those cheetahs he owns?* —J. G., SPOKANE, WASH.

A. No, it is not. Mr. McKay owns two cheetahs, all right—their names are Kenya and Spot—and he was indeed bitten—not by the cheetahs, but by, of all things, a small stray poodle! Mr. McKay, who is a fine animal person, saw the poodle, obviously lost in the middle of Sunset Drive, and went to rescue it. He did rescue it, too, but received a severe bite for his kindness. "But don't blame the dog," he told me quickly, "it was in the middle of traffic."

Gardner, incidentally, sent me a poem which went as follows:

DOG

A dog usually does what he sets out to do.
A dog can be introspective or outgoing.
A dog can look out a window longer than we can.
A dog does not worry about things he cannot control.
A dog does not speak.
A dog does not sweat.
A dog has better breath than we have.
A dog keeps his appearance up.
A dog does not lie or steal.
A dog studies bugs.

A dog gives us a look we interpret as love, though we might not look back.
A dog dies in agony every twelve seconds in a city pound.

Q. *I've seen Jim Fowler on shows with many different kinds of animals. What is his favorite?* —L. L., COLLEGE POINT, N.Y.

A. I put the question to my friend Jim this way. I asked him, if he had to be confined on a desert island with only one animal, which one would he choose? "An elephant," he told me. "They say if you raise an elephant for the first six months of its life, *he* may forget it but *you* won't." Fowler himself has a baby female elephant—she's seven—named Kontai, at his farm in Georgia. But I learned that the former (and still rerun) cohost of "Wild Kingdom" has had some kind of personal connection with just about every animal you can name. What, I asked him, was his first pet? "Well," he smiled, "There was this girl down the street named Susan. . . . No, seriously, my father was a soil surveyor, and he taught me to respect all living things. I was the kind of child a mother despairs of. When I was five, I had a whole family of possums. Possums, you know, are very difficult animals to raise."

Even in recent days, the six-foot six-inch former star athlete— he was once signed by the Philadelphia Phillies—has had trouble in this regard. His landlady in Chicago had posted a notice about pets in her building and called, suspiciously, on Jim. Quickly, he locked the door to his study, and welcomed the landlady to a seat on his living room sofa. Suddenly he noticed a peculiar look in her eye, and a deathly pallor. He looked around and saw that an eighteen-inch tongue had protruded out from under the study door and was exploring the other side. "What's that?" the landlady exclaimed. "Oh, that," replied Jim. "You said no dogs or cats. You didn't say anything about giant anteaters."

Q. *You say writers have always loved cats. Did any famous writers have famous cats?* —P. D., SAN MATEO, CALIF.

A. Yes, many of them did—practically all writers have loved to write about their cats. One of the most genuinely famous was

H. G. Wells's cat, Mr. Peter Wells, always known as Mr. Peter. He was best known for his comment to a guest in the house who talked either too long or too loudly. Mr. Peter would, with no small amount of cat theatrics, jump down from his chair and march—noisily, mind you—in the direction of the door. Have you ever heard a cat march noisily? Well, if you have, that cat is trying to tell you something.

Q. *I heard you tell a funny story about the Duke of Wellington and birds in a lecture. I think your readers would enjoy it.* —G. X., CLARION, PA.

A. It was a story about the Crystal Palace Exhibit in London and the problem, just before the opening, of how to get rid of all the sparrows inside the building. Queen Victoria decided to call in experts. Lord John Russell suggested a regiment of guards to shoot the sparrows, but Prince Albert vetoed this, pointing out that all the glass would be broken. Then Lord Palmerston was sent for. He proposed bird lime on the branches, but the prince vetoed this, too—the sparrows would merely move to other unlimed spots. Finally, the ultimate remedy was proposed: to send for the duke of Wellington. The hero of Waterloo duly appeared and took one look at the situation. "Oracularly," Cecil Woodham-Smith has recalled, "he uttered two words, 'Sparrow hawks.' " There was no need, however, for them. "At the sight of the Iron Duke," Lord Playfair recalled, "and the sound of the words 'Sparrow hawks,' the sparrows flew out of the Crystal Palace in a body and were never seen again."

Q. *I know Pablo Casals loved animals, and I understand he left a memorable statement about them. I have, however, never been able to find this.* —P. D., MIDDLETON, WIS.

A. The late Sr. Casals's statement is as follows: "There are, I know, people who do not love animals, but I think this is because they do not understand them—or because, indeed, they do not really see them. For me, animals have always been a special part of the wonder of nature—the smallest as well as the largest—with their amazing variety, their beautifully contrived shapes and fascinating habits. I am captivated by the spirit of them. I find in them a longing to communicate and a real capacity for love. If sometimes they do not trust but fear man, it is because he has treated them with arrogance and insensitivity." Sr. Casals himself, incidentally, had not only a covey of Great Danes; he was a cat man, as well.

Q. *Of our recent presidents, who really liked his pets best?* —G. C., STOCKBRIDGE, GA.

A. All of our recent presidents liked dogs. Even President Truman, not notably a pet owner, had a dog for a short time. Although FDR and Fala and Nixon and Checkers are famous public sagas, in my opinion the LBJ-Yuki relationship was the most touching. I know LBJ picked up his beagles by the ears, and he shouldn't have, but his grief at the death of Him, who was run over by Luci's chauffeur, was intense. And his love of Yuki, the little stray mongrel that Luci found abandoned at a gas station in Texas, was fully documented by Traphes Bryant, the famous White House dogkeeper.

On the cat side, Margaret Truman's book, *White House Pets*, states that many of our presidents kept felines—Abe Lincoln, Theodore Roosevelt and Calvin Coolidge, among others. Calvin Coolidge also owned a terrier, an Airedale, a collie, a sheepdog, two chow dogs, a bulldog, a police dog, three canaries, a pair of raccoons, a thrush, a goose, a donkey, a wallaby, a pygmy hippo, some lion cubs and a bear.

Calvin may have been "Silent Cal" with people, but with his animals he was very communicative.

Q. *All that praise for our presidents who liked dogs and cats! I'll bet you don't know which of our presidents was the greatest lover of horses.* —W. S., GAITHERSBURG, MD.

A. You lose. And by pure bad luck, because another reader sent me the inscription which one of our presidents wrote on the gravestone of his horse:

Here lies the body of my good horse, "The General." For 20
years he bore me . . . and in all that time never made a
blunder. Would that his master could say the same.

The president? John Tyler.

Q. *Jimmy Stewart is always in Westerns. Does he care about animals?* —D. W., PHILADELPHIA, PA.

A. I recently called on him at his house in Beverly Hills. On
the way to the living room he pointed out two enormous young
golden retrievers who seemed to be readying a charge through the
window. "And they've been to obedience school, too." Jimmy
shook his head. The dogs were now beating on the windowpanes.
How, we asked, did they do? Jimmy grinned. "*I,*" he said,
"learned a lot." Did he mean, we wondered, that he had gone, too?
"Yep," he admitted, "I missed 'em." He paused. "They let you
watch, you know, as long as you don't get near enough for 'em to
see you, and as long as you stay downwind of 'em.

"The other night," he said, as we sat down in the living room,
"Irene Dunne was sitting just where you're sitting. And the dogs
were all over her. She said she was allergic to them. And I
thought, 'Boy, I've really done it this time.' But the next day she
called and said she was fine—the dogs hadn't bothered her at all.
She even sounded concerned about them." He grinned again. "I
told her I was glad she was okay—but the dogs had been sneezing
quite a lot." He paused again and looked back at the dogs. "You
know," he said, "I got into the dog business when I married
Gloria." He caught himself. "Now that doesn't sound right, does
it? Anyway, I met her at a dinner party and I did the usual raised
eyebrow thing. And she was single and so I asked her if I could
take her home. When we got inside her door, though, a two-
hundred-pound German shepherd went for my jugular. Gloria did
a sort of baby-talk thing and then he laid down. From then on, he
just watched me and growled. I realized right then I'd have to win
the dog if I was ever going to win the girl. I did, too. Steaks from
Chasen's—the whole bit. And one day that dog came over and put
his head in my lap. And that, as I recall, was the day Gloria said
okay."

At this point Mrs. Stewart appeared on the scene. "Don't believe," she said, "a word of it. The only thing I ever did was get Jimmy outdoors. Me, a Brooklyn girl!" She showed us a picture she had taken of Ahmed, the late, great elephant of Kenya. It was an extraordinary picture. How far away were you, we asked. She pointed out the window. "About from here to the swimming pool," she said. Jimmy interrupted. "Honey," he said, "you're undercutting yourself. That swimming pool is half a mile away." Gloria laughed. "He's just promoting me," she said, "like he did my dog."

Q. *Yvette Mimieux seems to be "into" animals in a big way. True?*
—D. R., NORFOLK, VA.

A. True. The first time I ever met Miss Mimieux, ten years ago, she had a huge Great Dane named Sir Galahad and—now get this—a 200-pound jaguar named Zari. He had been given to her when he was just a baby. Sir Galahad and Zari were great friends, and Zari was pretty good with people, except that whenever anybody in the house took a bath, Zari used to want to take a bath too—in the same tub.

Today Miss Mimieux and her husband, Stanley Donen, have more reasonable pets, but she has not forgotten any of them. "I've had animals my whole life," she told me, "and I think I've had almost every kind of animal. When I lived in Mexico, I even had snakes. And I loved them, too."

Q. *Do any of the movie stars you write about really stand up for animals when it counts?* —D. B., TOLEDO, OHIO

A. Some not only stand up, they get mad, too. Rod McKuen, for example, shocked the august California Senate in Sacramento recently when, as vice president of the Fund for Animals, he testified for a bill to outlaw cruelty to animals in the filming of movies. He had just been asked by a senator why he was not equally interested in "people" causes, and Mr. McKuen, who is interested in many causes, was angry. "Sir," he said, "I was born a bastard. And that gives me an advantage over people who spend their lives becoming one."

The bill was, strangely, opposed by the American Civil Liberties Union, which never seemed to understand that what interested Mr. McKuen was not *what* was filmed, but *how* it was filmed. And, when we called on Mr. McKuen in his home, we found him angry about this also. "I wonder," he said, "if their idea of 'civil liberties' includes being tortured and killed for entertainment." For some time, we roamed around a home that includes a four poster bed, a six-by-four-foot TV screen, a small warehouse full of Mr. McKuen's books and a complete recording studio. Eventually we sat down among three Old English sheepdogs and several cats. Mr. McKuen stroked one of the sheepdogs, Mr. Kelly, named for his record-breaking stay at that emporium in Chicago.

"I must have," he told us, "the world's worst inferiority complex. I get into so many things—poetry, books, music, singing, composing, scoring. But I have only two projects I really care about—children and animals. I have been to too many orphanages ever to desert children, and as for my work with animals, I firmly believe that when we have no more animals to kill, we'll turn on each other. I've never met an animal I didn't like. I was bitten by a rattlesnake once, but later I got a pet rattlesnake, and I learned to love him. He just loved to be stroked."

Wild and Woolly

Q. *Which kind of animal do you most like just to watch?* —Y. C.,
BORDENTOWN, N.J.

A. This is going to surprise you, but I'm going to pick squirrels. I think watching them trying to decide whether to leap to the
next tree, or whether a little branch will hold them—watching
their whole decision-making process—well, to me, that's what a
love of animals is all about. But right up there with squirrels would
be cats. Some time ago, Eric Penick, the Notre Dame halfback, was
asked what he did in the summer. He replied that he ate a lot,
lifted weights and studied his cat, Panther. "Cats," he said, "have
the most beautiful moves of any animal. They never think about
it—they simply do it. I watch my cat all the time. I love to study
him. I try to pattern my moves after his. If I could run like a cat,
I'd be the greatest runner in the world."

Q. *How do birds fly? Also, how fast?* —P. A., LOGANVILLE, GA.

A. In brief, the fact that birds have maneuverable wings and
feathers makes flight possible. It's complicated, but the idea is that
the change in the position of the feathers causes a low-pressure area

in front of the bird, which makes it move forward, and another low-pressure area about its wings, which makes it move upward. As for speed, a racing pigeon has been clocked at seventy miles an hour for a five-hundred-mile race. However, the fastest birds have, in still air, gone as fast as one hundred miles an hour. And one thing is easy—to remember the name of the fastest bird. It's called a swift.

Q. *A friend told me that blind birds fly upside down. Is that possible?* —M. O., METAIRIE, LA.

A. It's not only possible, it's true. But your friend was probably talking about caged birds. Before flying to reach bars that are above them, these birds will usually flip over and fly upside down, the better to feel the bars, or for that matter, any obstruction, with their claws. Veterinarians tell me that blind fish also swim upside down—in their case, to feel the approach either of danger or of the surface.

Q. *Is it true you can keep sharks away by playing rock music at them?* —T. C., BRIDGEPORT, CONN.

A. You can even keep me away. Seriously, it is true. An Australian named Theo Brown actually worked on a kind of musical shark repellent. He discovered that when he played fox-trots or waltzes, the sharks came closer and closer, and couldn't get enough. But when he played a Beatles record, it was strictly see you later, alligator. Who says animals don't have good taste?

Q. *Are all animals color-blind?* —A. L., MASON CITY, IOWA

A. Put it this way: all mammals are, with the exception of man and monkey. Monkeys and apes are the only mammals, incidentally, which have really bright colors on their bodies—the bright blue and pink, for example, of the mandrill. Almost all birds can also distinguish colors, especially parrots and macaws, and other birds that, again, have bright colors themselves. However, as color authority David Gunston has pointed out, mammals do see quite clearly the difference in intensity of even blacks and whites. Thus, when you see a dog staring at, say, a girl's bright hair, what he is looking at is the hair's intensity, not its color. Or, to put it another way, does she or doesn't she? Only her parrot knows for sure.

Q. *Can you explain why our duck, who was hatched by the family hen, is convinced he's not a duck, but a chicken? He won't even associate with other ducks.* —T. C., WINFIELD, KANS.

A. Maybe he prefers to be henpecked, rather than duck-pecked. No, I'm kidding. Like the proverbial ugly duckling, your duck's confusion is the result of something called *imprinting:* with most birds, the first creature they see when they open their eyes—if the creature responds to them in some way—may well become their "parent" for life, and they think they are whatever species that parent is. The people in an artificial breeding program for whooping cranes, for example, created some startling problems for themselves when they did not at the outset recognize the power of the imprint phenomenon. The first batch of hand-raised cranes which were let loose took off and flew around for a while, but then descended on the first human beings they saw. These happened to be some people who were partaking of an outdoor barbecue. The barbecue almost immediately turned into an Alfred Hitchcock nightmare, and remember—whooping cranes are huge birds! With subsequent batches of baby cranes, the breeding programmers took stern measures. They disguised themselves with sheets and hoods and even went so far as to set up, in their nursery, larger-than-life cardboard cutouts of adult whooping cranes. Don't laugh—it worked!

Speaking of phony birds, the newest chapter in the age-old saga of the sportsman matching wits with "ferocious" wildlife is that of a "Trojan goose." That's right—a goose-blind built to resemble a large Canadian honker—one so large, in fact, that three hunters can fit inside. The migrating goose can see this blind from a long way off, and when this most interesting and sociable of birds approaches to find out what manner of giant comrade this is—well, put it this way: the goose finds out.

Q. *Which animals hibernate? For how long? Do they (a) eat, and (b) eliminate during that time?* —P. F., EATONTOWN, N.J.

A. People think bears and raccoons are the chief hibernators, but actually they're not—at least by strict hibernating standards. It's true they get awful sleepy during the winter and sleep a lot, but so do many other animals, like badgers and skunks. The chipmunk, for example, will take terrific naps during the winter, with a pile of nuts beside him. And he keeps waking up and eating them, though he's half-asleep. The real hibernators are woodchucks, marmots, hamsters, some squirrels, dormice, jumping mice, pocket mice and most reptiles. Hedgehogs hold the record; they even hibernate in captivity.

In real hibernation, an animal's body temperature goes down to a few degrees above freezing; the heartbeat can, for a squirrel, say, go from three hundred per minute to as low as ten, and during this period an animal can lose eighty percent of its weight. In real hibernation, too, animals neither eat nor defecate for the entire winter. On the other hand, when they wake up, their body temperatures may rise as much as eighty degrees in a few hours. Some animals aestivate—which means they sleep in the summer. Among them are crocodiles, alligators, snails, frogs and toads.

Some animals, among them certain kinds of squirrels and mice, have even been known to hibernate *and* aestivate—for which, the way man treats so many animals, you can hardly blame them. Now if they could figure out a way to take it easy in the fall and spring, they'd have—you'll pardon the expression—the game beat.

Q. *I'm tired of noisy, barking dogs. What is the quietest animal?*
—P. B., BOSTON, MASS.

A. Sshh, don't breathe a word. Have you thought of a leopard? I'm not serious, of course, but I've never forgotten reading about a leopard going by as "the flowing past of a phantom." The reason? It's feet have large, almost completely noise-muffling pads, yet it can hear at a truly amazing distance.

One writer recalls seeing a leopard two hundred yards away. Very quietly—so quietly the person beside him never even noticed he did it—he slipped his notebook out of his pocket. But the leopard did notice. The second he did it, the leopard's head went up and, in a bound, he was gone—obviously what we in the trade call a hard interview.

Q. *Which animals are the most monogamous?* —M. S., ARLINGTON, TEX.

A. As we mentioned before, the birds of prey—hawks, eagles, and so forth—are extremely monogamous. So are wolves; in fact, few wild, or for that matter domestic, animal families are more devoted. A few of the large cats—lynxes, mountain lions—also tend to stay together. But the most monogamous of all are geese and swans.

In fact, in 1959, in the Detroit River, when a female swan became frozen in the ice and had to be rescued and thawed out, all during the long rescue operation her mate refused to leave but swam around in a state of incredible distress. Finally, when the female was well enough to be let loose, as one writer put it, "the pair met, looked long at each other, then moved with that extra serenity downstream and out into Lake Erie."

Q. *Do any mammals live as long as man?* —H. B., LAS LUNAS, N. MEX.

A. Yes—elephants and whales. A female Asian elephant named Jesse, for example, lived in the Taronga zoo in Australia to the ripe old age of sixty-nine. And there have been instances, albeit rare, of whales living all the way to ninety. What kind of whales? Easy. Killer whales—which, by the way, don't.

Q. *Is it true Chicago was named for an animal? If so, what animal?* —E. H., NORTH CHATHAM, MASS.

A. It is, indeed. Chicago, or Sikako, was named for what the Cree Indians called the *sikak*, or skunk. And no other animal better illustrates the stupidity of humans toward them. We say "you skunk" as the lowest name-calling we can think of, and yet the skunk is not only among the most charming and amiable of all animals—one who uses his scent only as a last resort—but he is also the most valuable of all animals as a pest destroyer. He eats his weight several times a week in June bugs, potato bugs, mice and just about every other enemy the farmer has. In return, he's killed, cruelly trapped and called—well, a skunk.

Q. *You wrote that skunks are great animals. How about as pets?*
—F. A., WRAY, COLO.

A. Generally speaking, I am against wild animals as pets, period. However, there are exceptions, chief among which are wounded animals that, after being restored to health, are by then too domesticated to be returned to the wild. Among these the skunk ranks high—no pun intended. They are fun and friendly and fascinating and, even de-scented, brave.

But—and it is a big *but*—skunks are also difficult. If you don't believe it, try this story for size. Sloan Wilson, author of *The Man in the Gray Flannel Suit* and a close friend of mine, lives up in Ticonderoga, New York. Some time ago his daughter Jessica, age twelve, brought home a wounded skunk, Lilac, age undetermined. Lilac was soon restored to health but too domesticated to return to his earlier life. From the beginning, Lilac was crazy about Jessica. At the beginning, however, Lilac took a very dim view of Sloan.

"Why not?" Sloan told me. "Jessica is the permissive parent, I am a reasonable parent. Jessica felt Lilac could do anything he wanted to do. I felt Lilac could do *almost* anything he wanted to do. Jessica regarded Lilac as king of the roost. I regarded Lilac as an Indian 'man in a gray flannel suit': pure flannel on the outside, pure Indian in. 'Nonsense,' Jessica told me. 'You've got to learn to cooperate with Lilac.'

"My learning to cooperate," Sloan went on, "involved being bitten whenever and wherever Lilac wanted to bite. This was bad enough. But the real trouble came when Lilac fell in love with my shoe. It was not a one-night stand sort of thing. Interested in another shoe? No deal—he was faithful. I tried to give him my shoe. Again, nothing doing. It was not just the shoe he loved—it was the shoe and the animation of my foot inside it. My wife kept saying that skunks only have a three-week mating season, and just to be patient; but she wasn't the one being bitten. Skunks have very sharp teeth and biting was apparently a vital part of Lilac's passion. His teeth would go right through the shoe. I would push him off, I would throw him off, I would even, as gently as possible, try to kick him off. Nothing worked. Skunks are incredibly brave and persistent. There was no way I could intimidate him. The only way I could have gotten him to stop was literally to injure him."

The story, however, has a happy ending. Finally the three weeks were over and afterward—well, the story goes back to when Sloan was in the army, stationed in Greenland, and was attacked by a pack of starving huskies. To this day, when he's out walking, he remains unhappy about certain large dogs. But he now has the answer: he goes out for his walk with Lilac under his arm, and when an unfriendly dog appears, he calmly puts Lilac down. No matter what the size of the dog, he takes either one look or one sniff and hightails it in the opposite direction.

"It's funny," Sloan concluded, "you disarm them by de-scenting them, but they don't seem to know it and, more important, neither do their enemies."

Maybe, we hazarded, the dogs are just afraid Lilac will fall in love with them.

Q. *What is the most endangered animal of all?* —Q. B., MORRIS PLAINS, N.J.

A. My nomination would be the thylacine. Located in Tasmania, a kind of combination kangaroo and wild dog, this little fellow carries its young in a pouch but hunts like a coyote. It is believed there may be one or two lonely pairs still in existence, but no one has actually seen one in more than ten years.

Q. *You are always writing about animals that there are so few of left. What animal is there the most of?* —C. T., HATTIESBURG, MISS.

A. Good question. It's the beetle. In fact, two-thirds of all living creatures on earth are beetles. The heaviest insect in the world is a beetle: the Goliath beetle. He can weigh three and a half ounces and measure up to 6 inches. So is the smallest: a hairy winged little fellow who measures only .008 of an inch. Some kinds of beetles have incredible strength. Erma Reynolds, who is

an authority, declared one of these can support 850 times his own weight. If a man could do this he could lift sixty-three tons, yet the Olympic record for weight-lifting is only about one-fourth of one ton. Beetles can also be tough. The bombardier beetle, when attacked, emits a regular smoke screen to envelop his enemy. And as he does it you can hear a real bang.

Q. *What is the most ferocious animal in the world?* —D. W., HUNTINGTON, N.Y.

A. One of the last ones you would expect. In fact, though it is in many countrysides one of the commonest of all animals, it is also one which not one person in a hundred is aware of ever having seen. For one thing, it is an animal so tiny you would have to put two of them on a scale to register an ounce. Indeed, one member of its family is known as the smallest mammal of the world. For another thing, it moves so incredibly fast that, if you do see it, all you are likely to see is a furry little blur. It is—as you have probably guessed—the shrew, an animal which looks rather like a mouse with an elongated snout. It is literally afraid of nothing. It will eat an animal twice its own size and it will attack one ten times its own size.

Q. *You keep writing that dolphins are the most intelligent animals. How about chimpanzees?* —T. C., CASTLEWOOD, S.DAK.

A. I still go along with the dolphin, but I will agree that we are just beginning to understand how amazingly intelligent chimps are. The best example of this is a chimp named Washoe. Born in the wild, at ten months she came to the home of Drs. Allen and Trixie Gardner of Reno; and, in four years, she learned to "talk." What Washoe learned, however, was sign language, the Gardners having figured out that this would be easier for her. The story of how she learned was told on a public educational TV program, "Nova." Washoe not only has a large vocabulary, she plays games with words, invents new words and even, when there is nobody else around, talks to herself. You'll actually share the thrill when, seeing a duck for the first time, she gives the signs for "water bird." Or, even more incredible, when, seeing somebody has put a doll in her cup, she gives no less than four signs. "Baby," she says, "in my drink."

Q. *You wrote about the fastest animal in the world. What is the slowest?* —L. D., BOONE, N.C.

A. My nomination has got to be the sloth. He makes a turtle look like a speed-demon and a snail like a hot rod. He lives in the rain forests of South America's Amazon and Guiana valleys, and he has been called a masterpiece of immobility. Indeed, if you look closely at a sloth during the rainy season you may see tiny green plants on him—and they'll be growing, too! It can take a sloth two days to get from one tree to another. In the daytime he moves very little, and at night not a muscle. Gerald Durrell, who kept a family of sloths as pets, tested this by putting a plastic disk on a sloth's head in the early evening when he fell asleep. The next morning, he reported, it was still there.

But hold on now before you brand this little fellow one of the seven deadly sins. He isn't. He is a charming, endearing, peace-loving citizen who has a permanent smile on his face, awake or asleep. And he has good reason for his seemingly perpetual unmotion: his survival depends on his invisibility in foliage. Further-more, baby sloths are extremely energetic. Durrell recalls one whose greatest achievement was, as he puts it, "her solo ascent—without any equipment—of the sheer east wall of the bathroom. For steepness, smoothness and exposure," he says, "the Matterhorn pales in comparison."

Q. *Do canaries live wild anywhere? I would like to go study them.*
—S. A., MENA, ARK.

A. Canaries got their name from the Canary Islands, but the islands, ironically, didn't get their name from the birds.

The islands got their name from the Latin word *canis* ("dog") because they were inhabited by, according to the Elder Pliny, "a multitude of dogs of great size." And if you think I am going to argue with the Elder Pliny, you are mistaken.

However, as the Younger Amory, I am going to state that I believe it is very difficult today to find a wild canary anywhere, even on the Canaries, where the birds are generally grayish brown or olive green and a far cry—and song—from our domesticated yellow birds.

Our birds are the result of hundreds of years of selective breeding from finches captured in the Canaries in the sixteenth century, bred in Italy and carried to other parts of the world.

Incidentally, I believe in Henry David Thoreau's idea: if you want to study birds in the wild, how about not capturing *them* but going out to live among them and caging yourself?

Q. *Help, Mr. A! An animal needs your defense—and from the Bible (no less!). I quote the Book of Job, Chapter 39, about the female ostrich: "She is hardened against her young ones, as though they were not hers. . . . Because God hath deprived her of wisdom, neither hath He imparted to her understanding.* —S. J., TIPTON, IND.

A. One thing is sure: when it comes to battling against such utter untruths you need—well, the patience of Job. Not only is the female ostrich a good mother, so is the male. He travels with a brood of about six hens or so, who lay their eggs together in a pile. While the hens take turns sitting on the eggs in the daytime, the

male is the one who sits on them and guards them by night. And while we're at it, we might just as well lay that canard about being as foolish as an ostrich with its head in the sand: neither the female nor the male ostrich is foolish. They do not put their heads in the sand; they stretch their necks along the sand. While sitting on their eggs, this makes them, from a distance—even a short distance—almost indistinguishable from a hump in the sand or ground. The Bible, incidentally, is full of inaccuracies about animals.

Q. *Is the white tiger an albino?* —A. A., RAYNE, LA.

A. No, it is a mutant. An albino, dog or human or whatever, generally will have pink—or lack of pigmentation—in its eyes. There is also the question of whether albinos are capable of reproducing. Most albinos are sterile. The white tiger, in contrast, while it often has some visual problems, is actually bigger and stronger than the regular striped tiger and, furthermore, it lives longer. The average tiger's life span, in protected areas, at least, is twenty years. The two white tigers now on loan from the National Zoo to the Brookfield Zoo in Chicago are twenty-six years old.

In 1951 the Maharajah of Rewa found the only white tiger ever discovered in the wild. He mated it with a striped tiger. The first litter of this match was all striped, but all the cubs still had the white recessive genes. And, true to the laws of heredity, when these offspring had offspring, they produced another white. Then this white and the original white also mated and they produced another all-white.

But how valuable the white tigers are—there are thirty-five in the world—is evident from the fact that the Miami zoo proposed an exchange with the Indian zoological people on the basis of one white tiger for two leopards and two cheetahs. Unlike a baseball trade, however, there was no outfielder to be named at a later date.

Q. *Someone told me that bees are mini–sun worshippers, and that they perform dances and rituals in the direction of the sun. True or false?*
—S. F., SUMMERVILLE, S.C.

A. A little of both, actually. Bees do dance, and the dances are concerned with the position of the sun, but it's no mere ritual. A bee who has been out on a foraging expedition and who has found a good source of food makes a beeline back to the hive, calls the other bees together, and proceeds to give detailed directions to the location of the goodies. First he points his body to the sun, then he performs a number of turns and pirouettes to draw a pattern that, in bee language, indicates the direction and distance to go. He repeats this several times; and while he is dancing, he is also tracing his dance with a secretion which will act as a record that other bees will follow when they come by later.

But now we come to the really uncanny stuff. A bee who reads the record, for example, four hours later, not only takes into consideration the age of the message but also calculates where the sun was four hours before and adjusts his flight direction accordingly. More incredible still, bees in experiments have been kept in totally sunless rooms, given a food source and then, while researchers waited for what they thought would be total confusion, the bees instead promptly bestowed the total confusion on them. The scout bees, who had found the food, came back to the group, performed the dance as usual and gave the exact directions, according to the position of the sun outside.

Q. *I have a question that nobody seems to be able to answer. Why do bees die after they sting someone?* —S. C., MONTREAL, QUE.

A. Worker bees do die, queen bees don't. When the worker bee stings what to her is relatively thick skin, like a person's, the barbs on her stinger catch. In her struggle to free them, she will usually break her stinger, and the breaking of this so injures her that the chances are she will die.

The queen bee, however, has an easier stinger to get in and out and does not die. But the fact is, she does not use her stinger to defend—all she uses it on are other, rival queens!

Q. *I have heard that only the female wasp stings. (a) Is this true, and (b) how can I tell the female from the male?* —P. H., NEWTON, MASS.

A. (a) It is true; (b) look it in the eye. Seriously, a stinger is really part of the female wasp's egg-laying apparatus. The male will pretend he can sting—and even go through the motions—but he can't. And you really can tell the difference by the eyes. The male has light-colored eyes, the female dark-colored. The male has a yellow forehead, too, and yellow legs and undersides. The female is dark. Of course, if you want to know how you can look this closely at a wasp and not get stung if it is a female—well, that's a good question. Next question, please.

Q. *Everybody says somebody—always somebody else—drinks like a fish.*
Seriously, do fish drink? In salt water? —D. M., SANTA ROSA, CALIF.

A. Yes, sea-water or salt-water fish do drink—and like fish,
too. They take in large quantities of salt water through their
mouths, and then excrete the salt through cells in their gills or as
waste from their very efficient kidneys. On the other hand, the
fresh-water fish face the problem of the sea-water fish in reverse.
They don't drink through the mouth at all—in fact, they take in
water through their surface tissues and are constantly in danger of
flooding—drowning—except for the fact that they also have very
efficient kidneys that work overtime getting rid of the excess water.

Q. *I have heard that lions are wanton killers and also man-eaters. Is*
this true? —N. J., PATERSON, N.J.
A. Far from it. A pride of lions, six or more, kill on the
average two meals a week—antelope, zebra, and so on—and almost
never kill between meals. As for the man-eating claims, almost all
of them turn out, when run down, to be man-made myths. There

were, however, two maneless lions at Tsavo who did kill many workers during the construction of a railroad through their domain in the Kenya bush. And, of course, the legend of lions eating Christians—which was, after all, hardly the lions' fault—persists.

Our favorite story is the one about the missionary who, as he was walking in Africa, heard the ominous padding of a lion behind him. "O Lord," prayed the missionary, "grant in Thy goodness that the lion walking behind me is a good Christian lion." And then, in the silence that followed, the missionary heard the lion praying, too. "O Lord," he prayed, "we thank Thee for the food which we are about to receive. . . ."

Q. *My friend is trying to tell me there's a fish that walks. Come on!*
—R. K. (AGE NINE), GLADSTONE, ORE.

A. Come on where? If you want to go as far as the Amazon River basin in South America, then you would indeed see one. It's called the walking catfish of the Amazon. Known in scientific circles as *pterygoplichthys multiradiatus* (but you can call him pterry for short), this big fish, which, since he's covered with bony plates, is also called the armored catfish, has a way of swimming up over the banks of the river when the Amazon floods in spring. Thus he is often left, when the waters recede in late summer, surrounded by dry land. Since he can survive for a short period of time while breathing air, he merely rises up on his spines, turns his tail toward the ground and, supported this way, strolls back home.

Q. *You've written about animals like skunks and coyotes being maligned. How about the lowly octopus?* —M. H., STONINGTON, CONN.

A. You are so right. I am convinced that, of all the beasts of the sea, not one is more maligned than the octopus. From its very name—it has been called devilfish—all the way back through history, it has had a terrible press. Victor Hugo, for example, wrote as follows: "The tiger can only devour you, but the devilfish inhales you. He draws you into him, bound and helpless. To be eaten alive is more than terrible; to be drunk alive is inexpressible."

There isn't an iota of truth here. The plain fact of the matter is that the octopus is deadly afraid of anything larger than he is. When an enemy frightens him, incidentally, he turns pale, and, if really terrified, he can apparently turn from color to color.

Q. *Senator Sam J. Ervin, Jr., said in the Watergate hearings that lightning bugs carry their lights behind them. Is this true? And what is the difference between a lightning bug and a firefly?* —A. O., PROSPERITY, W. VA.

A. Actually, what they do is hide their lights under a bushel. They carry their lights underneath, rather than behind—on the undersides of their stomachs.

There is no difference between a lightning bug and a firefly— and both are, in reality, beetles. The males use their lights to attract females. They fly slowly near the ground and flash on an average of once every 5.8 seconds. From the grass, the female flashes back—exactly 2.1 seconds afterward. If you don't believe it, naturalist Donald Culross Peattie suggests you time it. Put a flashlight in the grass and signal every 2.1 seconds—oh, the heck with it, make it every 2 seconds—and you'll be surprised at the results.

And never underestimate the power of a firefly's light. In the Spanish-American War, in 1898, Dr. William Gorgas, of Panama Canal fame, was operating on a soldier when his light went out. Using the light of a bottle full of fireflies, he successfully completed the operation! Fireflies are even used in romance. The girls of Brazil, for example, are given to putting fireflies in their hair. And they attract males, too—although not, presumably, every 2.1 seconds.

Q. *I want to ask you about an animal I've never been able to find in any zoo: the duckbilled platypus. And it's supposed to be the "missing link," too. Missing, between what? Us and apes?* —S. A., HAMDEN, CONN.

A. No; basically, between us and fish—between land and water life. The duckbilled platypus is the perfect amphibian: a fur-bearing little fellow about the size of a muskrat, and with claws; but he lays eggs, his feet are webbed, and he's got that duck mouth. Also, he's the only mammal that, although he's a playful fellow, can poison you. On his rear ankles are spurs from which he can exude venom. The reason you've never seen any in zoos is that, though they have existed for fifty million years, a few years ago they were almost totally destroyed for—you guessed it—the fur. Now they are so rigidly protected by the Australian government that even zoos can't get them. The Bronx zoo once had two, but the last disappeared under mysterious circumstances—in other words, was probably stolen. If so, the thief got a handful. The platypus eats twenty-five thousand worms a month—and that's only part of his diet.

Q. *I have three questions about kangaroos: (a) do they really box? (b) how do their babies get in their mothers' pouches? and (c) what do people kill them for?* —N. G., LEAD, MONT.

A. (a) Yes and no. Trained kangaroos box but wild ones don't. Male kangaroos in the wild confront each other by rearing up on their hind legs, using their tails for balance, and, though they seem to be using their short front legs or forearms as a boxer would, in reality they use them to hold the opponent preparatory to giving him a swift kick. Male kangaroos, like most male animals, do not, contrary to what you may have read, fight bloodthirsty battles to the death. In fact, the only recorded instance of a fight between two male kangaroos in which the loser died of injuries occurred in a zoo.

(b) The journey of the baby kangaroo to its mother's pouch is one of the most extraordinary wonders of nature. The baby kangaroo at birth is less than an inch long—no bigger than a bee—and yet, at that tiny size, with no toes yet on its hind feet, and using only its forefeet or little "hands," it must undertake all alone, although it is still attached by a thread of an umbilical cord, the most important journey of its life. It takes about three minutes for it to get to the pouch, where the mother's teats are, and where it will stay for about six months.

(c) The Australians kill kangaroos to make everything from athletic shoes to kangaroo-tail soup.

Q. *Is it true that when sea gull babies are hungry, they tap on a red spot on their parents' beaks? Is it true they won't strike another gull when he has his head down?* —S. M., ELBRIDGE, N.Y.

A. Yes, both are true. In fact, Mrs. H. Jean George, who had a pet sea gull who wouldn't eat, actually got him to eat by the red-spot route. She put some lipstick on her thumb and held it over the gull. Immediately the gull struck the spot, and afterward opened his mouth—whereupon Mrs. George fed him. And sea gulls do indeed have a code about not hitting a fellow gull unless his head is up. Head-up neck-stretching is a sea gull status thing, and even a tough male gull, when walking across another gull's territory, keeps his head down.

Q. *What is the correct pronunciation of* koala? *What does it mean? Is it a real bear? Is it endangered?* —N. F., LA CROSSE, WIS.

A. It is pronounced ko-*a*lla. It's an aboriginal word meaning "no drink." Eucalyptus is his water. Although the koala looks like a Teddy—Theodore Roosevelt—bear, and may well have been the model for that world-famous toy, the fact remains that it is not a bear—it is a true marsupial. The female carries her young in her pouch for about six months, and then on her back, piggy-back style, for six more. One woman in Australia had a pet orphan koala; the only place it was happy was piggy-back on her head.

Finally, the koala is indeed endangered. Although it is one of the most trusting of all wild creatures, it is also one of the most helpless: it can neither fight nor run; in 1924, the high tide of the so-called koala bearskin craze, almost two million were killed. Now they're protected, and when Jacqueline Kennedy asked for a pair for White House pets, she was told, "Sorry, not even for you." Nor do they any longer make Teddy or toy koala bears out of koala skins. So what do they make them out of? Kangaroo skins—which, of course, are also endangered.

Q. *Do flying squirrels really fly? I've seen them, and they really do have wings.* —E. N., PARMA HEIGHTS, OHIO

A. No, they do not fly—they glide. They don't have wings, either. What you think is their wings is actually part of their skin, which, since it is quite loose and seems to have an extra section stretching from their front paws to their back paws, acts as a wing.

They also use their tails as a kind of rudder. In any case, from an elevation of 60 feet, they have been known to glide over 150 feet—half the length of a football field! Then why haven't more people seen them? It's all because, according to Anne La Bastille, who has long studied flying squirrels, they are the most nocturnal of all American mammals. Ms. La Bastille also maintains that flying squirrels are terrific animal mothers—the mother doesn't shove her young flying fry out of the nest and just let them fly or fall, or anything as tough as that. Instead, she glides with them on short hauls until they are able to solo.

Q. *Is there really such a thing as a* white *rhinoceros?* —I. C., SEWICKLEY, PA.

A. Of courseros. Actually, the phrase *white rhinoceros* is a mispronunciation of *wait rhinoceros*—the old Boer description of a wide-mouthed species of rhino. The white rhino doesn't have the long upper lip of the black rhino and is also a very gentle fellow. Rarely will he charge. The white rhinoceros, like its cousin, the black rhinoceros, is grayish tan in color—and, when it has been having a delicious roll in the mud, considerably darker than that.

Q. *Why do beavers build dams? Do they really mate for life?* —J. G., BOARDMAN, OHIO

A. Once upon a time, it was thought beavers built dams—you will excuse the expression—just for the hell of it. Now it is known they build dams for a very good reason: for protection from the winter. Winter, for the beaver, means no open water. He can't safely trek over ice and snow for his food. So, from a stream, small or large, he makes a pond. He uses this pond for two things: first, on its mud bottom, to anchor his winter food supply (bark and timber); and second, just over the high-water mark of the pond, to build his house. This house, which has an underwater door for protection, as well as an above-water one, may actually be connected with the dam, or it may not be. But one thing is certain: colonies of beavers together have built some incredibly large dams. The record was one in Montana, which was almost half a mile in width. And beavers do indeed mate for life. At a recent meeting of American and Russian environmentalists, V. V. Krinitsky, leader of the Russian delegation, declared movingly, "When the male and female beavers who mate for life are forced apart, they cry as we would."

Q. *Somebody told me the most trapped animal in this country is the nutria. What on earth is a nutria?* —F. S., SHERMAN OAKS, CALIF.

A. The nutria is an animal which, ironically, originally started out to be ranched. A native of South America known as the South American beaver, he is a strange-looking fellow, something like a king-sized guinea pig, with teeth like Bugs Bunny and front and back feet which don't even match: his front feet, with four toes, are paws; his back feet, with five, are webbed. A pair was brought over to Louisiana in the 1930s as a ranch experiment, and during a hurricane managed to escape from their "escape-proof" pen. Immediately they headed for the bayous, and ever since, they have been trapped in tremendous numbers for their beautiful and extremely versatile pelts. Last year trappers trapped almost two million of them.

Q. *Germany's Marshal Rommel was called "the Desert Fox." Is there such an animal?* —F. H., COLONIA, N.J.

A. There is indeed; in fact, several kinds. In the southern part of Africa, for example, there is the African sand fox. In the north, there are two others: Ruppell's fox, which has pretty big ears; and also a fascinating little fellow called a fennec, which has truly enormous ears. Indeed, it has, for its size, the biggest ears of any animal. But the fennec's huge ears serve a purpose: the little guy has to exist in extraordinarily high temperatures, and his ears are part of his excellent excess radiation system. Lois Bueller, in *Wild Dogs of the World*, tell how one man in Paris made pets out of a couple of fennecs and kept them in his apartment. In the daytime, he found them gentle, fastidious and even easy to housebreak. At night, however—they are, after all nocturnal animals—he found them holy terrors. At last report, he was looking for night-work.

Q. *How come the expression, crocodile tears? Crocodiles don't cry.*
—L. H., CHULA VISTA, CALIF.

A. Like so many animal expressions, this one—for hypocritical grief—has no basis in fact. Indeed, since the idea comes from two canards—(a) that crocodiles cry in order to lure nearby people to them so that they may eat them, and (b) that they themselves shed tears over their prey while they're eating it—it is not once but twice removed from the truth. Crocodiles have, in fact, no tear glands and therefore do not "cry" in that sense at all. They should, however, be able to—over what has been done to them. No animal has been more severely poached, and the irony is that the poachers use just the skin of their stomachs for leather; the rest of the animal is thrown away. Now there are so few left that even the poachers can't find them.

Q. *I've heard somebody found a real dragon on an island somewhere. Is it true?* —P. B., COQUILLE, ORE.

A. Yes, only it wasn't a *dragon*, of course—that's a word that has no zoological meaning. It was a huge lizard, eleven feet long and weighing four hundred pounds, and was found and photographed on the Indonesian island of Komodo. Here's an eyewitness report from the photographer, Peter Arnold, in *Animals* Magazine:

> *We were no more than six feet from them when suddenly the ground shook. An enormous dragon crashed through the undergrowth and stopped abruptly when he reached the edge of the clearing. Sitting on his haunches like a dog, he looked around at the situation.*
>
> *He was a ten-foot monster, darker in color than the younger dragons, his grotesque scaly hide hanging from his bulky body as if too big for him. He made a low hissing sound, then lurched forward like a tank, carrying his heavy tail high off the ground. The smaller dragons hurried off. The dominant male approached the bait (and us), his long yellow tongue darting out and in.*
>
> *At the moment, I believed all the fables of twenty-three-foot monsters and the stories of man-eating and even fire-breathing dragons.*

You'll be glad to know the Indonesian government has proclaimed Komodo a Dragon Sanctuary. So let's not hear any nonsense about some hunter slaying a dragon.

Q. *I've heard that whales and dolphins navigate by sonar! Is this really true?* —L. W., WILLOW, N.Y.

A. It is indeed true. Ocean mammalogists who have long puzzled over the ability of dolphins and certain species of whales to navigate, as well as to communicate with each other over vast areas, now believe that the answer may lie in an unltrasophisticated sonarlike system which these fascinating creatures carry, built-in, in their heads. But, if you think that's something special, how about salmon or—better yet—green sea turtles? Born on tropical island beaches, the green sea turtles have been known to return for egg-laying not just to the same island but even to the same beach— and this without, as far as man can discover, any special kind of homing system at all.

According to Richard Perry in *Life at the Sea's Frontier*, Costa Rican green sea turtles, for example, making their way to their feeding grounds in the sea immediately after birth, take in a two-thousand-mile range, from Cuba to the Yucatan in Mexico. Then, when their own egg-laying time approaches, these same turtles come back not just to their Tortuguero Beach in Costa Rica, but, on some occasions, to within a quarter of a mile of their own birthplaces. Homecoming, it appears, is not just for college alumni and football teams.

Q. You write about how great so many animals are. What about minks? You must admit they have very little to recommend them. Believe me, I know firsthand that they would as soon bite you as breathe. —H. D., CLAYTON, MO.

A. If I were a mink, I'd think human beings had pretty little to recommend them. After all, humans do one of two things to them: either torture them to death in traps or imprison them for life in cages. And all for what? Vanity—for themselves. Furthermore, that male minks, if allowed to get together on a mink ranch, will murder each other, or that female minks, when agitated, will often kill their young, still proves nothing. How would human beings behave under similar conditions? Probably they wouldn't have the courage to kill their young to spare them such a life. And remember something else. Mink mothers, it is true, are often accused of not caring for their young. Yet mink mothers have been known, when their milk ran short, to allow their kits to eat them alive.

Q. *You recently wrote about the most playful wild animals. What about prairie dogs?* —M. S., WHITE SULPHUR SPRINGS, W. VA.

A. You are right—I forgot them. As a matter of fact, there is an incident on record of a colony of prairie dogs playing an actual game of Prisoner's Base. The way they did it in this case was that one prairie dog ran toward another prairie dog's hole. Then still a third prairie dog ran toward the first's hole. The first one started back; meanwhile, others joined the game, until the whole colony was doing it. And, according to my information, nobody dogged it, not even the prairie prisoners at the base, who squealed and howled encouragement. There was even blocking and tackling.

Q. *I am taking my family on a Western vacation by automobile. I love prairie dogs and I want to see a prairie-dog town. Where should I go?* —Y. L., DARLINGTON, S.C.

A. The best place is Alcalde, New Mexico, near Santa Fe. There the U.S. Department of Interior has set up a Prairie Dog Town, complete with roadsigns, as a tourist attraction. Another good bet is a seven-acre Dog Town in Lubbock, Texas. But you had better hurry. President Ford gave in to ranchers and livestock interests and rescinded President Nixon's ban on poisoning on public lands. The prairie dog's days, like those of so many other wild animals of the West, may be numbered.

At either of these locations, you will see fascinating sights. When prairie dogs meet each other around their burrows, they exchange a real "kiss"—it may last as long as ten seconds—actually touching mouths and teeth. It's their way of identifying members of their own burrow. Strangers are chased away, with one important exception: if they are being pursued by a coyote or other predator, they will receive sanctuary.

The burrows themselves are among nature's wonders. The main entrances have mounds that serve both to keep out water and as observation posts. Inside, the burrows tunnel down seven or eight feet, and then the tunnels turn upward—again to avoid flooding—and might continue on for as much as eighty feet. Along the way are listening posts, guard rooms, sleeping chambers, nurseries and, of course, quick-escape routes.

Q. *Why do people say he or she eats like a bird? It seems to me birds eat a lot.* —H.W., PEBBLE BEACH, CALIF.

A. People shouldn't say it—and birds do eat a lot. If you don't believe it, read this slowly. To eat proportionately as much as a hummingbird, a man would have to consume 285 pounds of meat or 370 pounds of boiled potatoes—every day!

Q. *I have three questions about mosquitoes. Why do they lay eggs underwater? How long do they live? And are they good for anything?* —P. F., HENDERSON, COLO.

A. Well, they don't lay eggs underwater; they lay eggs on the surface of the water. Female mosquitoes live about ten days. The male, however, lives only eight or nine. And he, as we've told you, is the one who doesn't bite! Finally, they are good for something. They're good food for animals, birds, fish and other insects, many of which, if they don't have mosquitoes to eat, might perish and allow proliferation of even worse pests than mosquitoes.

Q. *Do peacocks really dance?* —T. P., BRUNDIDGE, ALA.

A. Indeed they do—haven't you ever heard of peacock-in-the-straw? Seriously, the mating dance of this glorious bird has entranced naturalists for years. And the female of the species doesn't even have to be around when the dance begins! Wildlife photographer Jack Denton Scott once sat in a tree-blind in India waiting to photograph a tiger when he was mesmerized by the sight of a dozen young peacocks who, and I quote, "strutting and bowing, paired off. First there was a forward dance," Mr. Scott writes, "then an equally graceful backward movement, which was almost a rhumba." As if that weren't enough, peacocks are not always, apparently, attracted to peahens. There is a Bronx zoo legend, possibly apocryphal, of a domesticated peacock named Lucifer who fell in love with, of all things, a turtle named Geraldine. For three years, so the story goes, Lucifer lived with Geraldine in her turtle yard, and their connubial bliss was only disturbed when Lucifer was displaced, not by another turtle but by—you guessed it—another peacock, named Oswald.

Q. *Does a camel's hump actually store water? Why do they have such mean dispositions?* —F. D., MENTOR, OHIO

A. No. A camel's hump may contain as much as a hundred pounds of fat, but this fat supplies energy, not water. Anyway, when it does get to drink, the camel drinks an amazing amount: twenty-seven gallons in ten minutes. This water, however, doesn't stay in its stomach, but passes into its tissues. When it can't drink, the animal draws upon the fat in its hump.

In any case, the camel's endurance is legendary. It can move along at seven or eight miles an hour for as long as eighteen hours straight.

It has what you describe as a mean disposition for darn good reasons. It has been mistreated for thousands of years.

It also has a good memory. There is a well-known story of an Arab driver who unmercifully beat his camel. The camel could do—and did—nothing about it. Two days later, however, by which time the driver was completely off-guard, the camel got him—with one kick. Its kick is a very formidable weapon, indeed.

Q. *How do porcupines mate?* —E. C., WILMINGTON, DEL.

A. Very carefully. No, that is an old joke; almost as old as the old Indian belief that the female porky hangs upside down on the underside of a small branch. Actually porcupines mate like any other quadrupeds. Only in fear and rage do the porky's quills become formidable weapons; otherwise they lie lengthwise and harmless along the porky's back and sides.

Q. *I've heard that penguins have a really low divorce rate. Is this true?* —M. N., UTICA, N.Y.

A. It is indeed true. Richard Penney, who has spent many years studying the Adélie penguins in the Antarctic, has reported that in his particular group of penguins at Wilkes Station, the percent of adults which mated one year and then returned the next to the same mate was eighty-four. In other words, a sixteen percent divorce rate.

And, remember, life for the Adélie is not easy. He and his

mate have been separated for seven months, and have traveled, separately, as much as nine hundred miles. Because of the high death rate due to storms and being eaten by their enemies, often there will be no returning male—or female.

When the latter happens, the male will try to court another, he by dropping a pebble carried in his beak at the feet of his love, she by picking up the pebble and starting a nest. Sometimes there are two females who want the same pebble, and then look out! The female is not only more deadly than the male when it comes to protecting her nest, she is also more deadly at, well, feathering it.

Q. *I often find baby wild animals. What should I feed them?*
—C. K., CAMBRIDGE, MASS.

A. The first thing you should do is make sure the animal really is abandoned; sometimes the mother is near and waiting for you to go away. When you're sure it's abandoned, or lost, and you don't know exactly what kind of animal it is, you're always safe with warm milk, baby cereal and eggs—both cooked and raw. According to a new book, *Care of the Wild*, by Mae Hickman and Maxine Guy, for the very young who have not yet opened their eyes, you should use a nursing bottle (available at pet stores) or an eyedropper (not glass—their sharp teeth may break it off) and feed the following formula: 3 ounces homogenized milk, a teaspoon of baby cereal, a drop of corn syrup, a touch of calcium gluconate, a drop of vitamin oil, a few drops of wheat germ oil and ½ teaspoon Esbilac (available at your vet's or local drugstore). This book, *Care of the Wild*, is terrific about how to rescue and treat different animals and different animal injuries. It's available for $4 from Unity Press, P. O. Box 1037, Santa Cruz, California 95060.

Q. *You were quoted as saying any animal is capable of giving and receiving affection, and won't necessarily harm man. Do you include bears?*
—F.M., RAVENNA. OHIO

A. I do indeed. In fact, I give you a remarkable story, told by an outdoorsman, Bob Leslie. He lived with wild creatures of all kinds for more than thirty years. One day he was fishing when a huge black bear approached him. The bear sat down on his haunches less than five feet away. Leslie respected what he calls the "first fear" of wild creatures—sudden movement—and made none. Instead, when shortly he had caught a fish, he tossed it to the bear. He did this again and again. He also noticed that the bear did not make any attempt to grab any fish until Leslie had it off the line; instead, the bear watched the process intently. "His patience and dignity," said Leslie, "were regal."

That began an amazing saga that went on for many days. The bear and the man literally lived together. At night, when it rained, the bear would come inside Leslie's lean-to and sit or lie right beside him. When the bear licked his hand, Leslie would go and get him a handful of salt. When the bear indicated an itch, and where, Leslie would scratch.

They even wrestled together, and although the bear weighed five hundred pounds and could literally "gallop," as Leslie puts it, to the top of a tree, the bear never injured him except once, in exuberance, and afterward was so upset he came and licked his face. If the game got too rough, Leslie would lie motionless and again the bear would lick. Odd things scared the bear—thunder and lightning, for one, as well as whiskey jacks and other birds. Leslie comforted him at such times, and one evening both bear and man stared into each other's eyes for a long period. "I felt an awed humility," Leslie wrote, "as if the Diety Himself were about to effect a revelation through this, another of his children."

After one such time, as suddenly as he had first come, the bear disappeared—forever.

Q. *What does a coyote eat?* —H. C., LOGAN, UTAH

A. Anything that doesn't eat him first. No, actually, and in keeping with his position as America's most valuable predator, his diet consists primarily of such animals as mice, moles, gophers and rabbits. I have called him the little brother of the wolf, yet he is also a close cousin of the dog—as witness the coyote in Phoenix who went into the trailer of a computer technician and jumped right in his lap to be petted.

No other animal has all three senses—sight, smell and hearing—as keen as his. Basically monogamous, coyotes mate for long periods, if not for life. And when two unmated males fight for the same unmated female, after it is over she is very likely to choose not the one who won, but the one who lost. As for the male, when his mate is pregnant he will not eat until she has. And when she gives birth, he stands guard over the den. When the female leaves the den, he cares for the pups.

This is the animal which is so unmercifully, by day and by night, all year long, hunted, trapped, "denned" and poisoned. All because of monstrous lies about an "annual sheep destruction of 800,000."

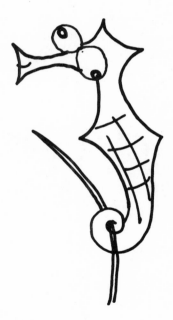

Q. *Is there any such thing as a sea horse?* —R. D., HAZELHURST, GA.

A. If I say so, there is. No, I'm kidding. But there actually is. In fact there are no less than forty different kinds of sea horses. They live in a lot of places, too—Hawaii, the Indian Ocean, even parts of the Mediterranean—practically anywhere, indeed, where there is warm water. My favorite description of them is from a writer named Deena Clark. They have, she said, "the arched neck and head of a stallion, the swelling bosom of a pouter pigeon, the grasping tail of a monkey and the color-change power of a chameleon." If that isn't enough for you, they also have eyes which can work independently of each other. One can be looking at the surface, while another can be looking underwater.

If you still don't think these horses (which, incidentally, can't swim very well) aren't something else, try this: they have a kangaroo kind of pouch for their babies. And you know who has this pouch? Not the female, but the male. In fact, the female not only pursues the male and transfers her eggs into his pouch in their mating dance, she also goes off and leaves him for forty or fifty days to do the dirty work.

Q. *You recently wrote about frogs. Where does the word* toady *come*

from—as in the expression, Toady to the rich? —N. T., FRAMINGHAM, MASS.

A. It comes, strangely enough, from the day when toads were regarded as poisonous, and nobles had their "toad eaters"—actually people who ate toads, in other words, poison—or at least pretended to eat them, to "save the lives" of their masters. In time, it was applied to any flatterer who would say anything to please someone powerful.

Q. *What is the difference between a turtle and a tortoise?* —T. M., COVINGTON, TENN.

A. A turtle lives in the water, and a tortoise on the land. Generally speaking, there are two kinds of turtles: pond and river turtles, and sea turtles. The latter are very different looking from tortoises, having, among other features, webbed feet and flippers.

Q. *Is it true that an eagle, if it is attacked on the ground, lies on its back and fights with its claws?* —D. H., NASHVILLE, TENN.

A. It is indeed true. The eagle's talons, claws or feet, depending on what you want to call them, are his most powerful weapons, and if he can't take to the air and is surprised on the ground, that is the way he will fight. The grip of an eagle is so strong that even the most powerful person, caught by an eagle's toe, could not loosen it.

Q. *You said a sea lion would have no trouble beating Mark Spitz; that a sea lion went 25 miles an hour and Spitz, setting the world's record, only 4.31 miles an hour. How about a dolphin?* —V. N., GAKONA, ALASKA

A. A dolphin would leave the sea lion tied to a post. Dolphins have been clocked at over 35 miles an hour. They overtake and keep ahead of ocean liners. The reason—the dolphin's whole body undulates. The friction of his body is ten percent of Mr. Spitz's. And, as I indicated before, on television Mr. Spitz's is even higher.

Q. *What animal is the most difficult to train?* —G. T., JOPLIN, MO.

A. You would never guess this one. It is, of all animals, the zebra! Indeed, the zebra is practically the only animal that never appears in any kind of act. Why? Well, the animal encyclopedias tell you it's because they are terrible-tempered and mean. We don't buy that; and even if we did, if we were a zebra, faced with what man has done to the species (using him for everything from rugs to coats to flyswatters), we'd be mean, too. Anyway, there is only one circus act in existence that uses zebras. And—hold your hat—the animals in that act aren't really zebras, after all. They're painted ponies.

Q. *Do you believe there is such a thing as "affection" training?* —N. T., FREEPORT, TEX.

A. Yes, I do, and Ralph Helfer and his wife, Toni, the two animal trainers who are generally credited with starting it, are my principal reasons for so believing. When they were working on the "Daktari" TV series, all their animals—lions, tigers, and everything—were up in "Africa, U.S.A." in Saugus, outside Los Angeles, when there was a terrible flash flood. The only way to save the animals was to turn them loose. Had they not been "trained" and trained kindly, they would have panicked, and fought each other, not to mention the keepers who were trying to save them. Instead they saved human as well as animal lives —Helfer himself rescued one baby tiger by swimming out while holding onto an elephant's tail.

Helfer now operates what he calls "The Home of Affection Training"—an animal park in Buena Vista, called "The Enchanted Village." He told me that affection training was born twenty-five years ago in a hospital bed—i.e.:

> *Violence begets violence, I mused as I lay in my hospital bed twenty-five years ago, after being mauled by a 500-pound lion. The big cat had been "fear trained" with whips, chairs, and screams—as animals in captivity traditionally are—and though he performed his tricks well enough, he had no love for humans. Just as a battered child grows up to become a child abuser, a battered animal awaits his chance to do unto others as has been done unto him. I had been done unto royally by that lion, and I had plenty of time during a long convalescence to figure out why. That lion had attacked me, as so many other animals have attacked humans over the centuries, not because he was "wild," but because he was unloved. Your dog or cat is no different—nor is your horse or fish or pig or bird.*
>
> *The idea of affection training was born in that hospital bed. Animals respond to their lives emotionally, I reasoned. If an animal could be trained by addressing his negative emotions (with threats and punishment), he could probably also be trained by appealing to his positive emotions. Surely the results would be even better with love than with pain, for the animal would be motivated to cooperate. Where pain might get the horse to water, love could induce him to drink.*
>
> *Since that time I've proved my theory with almost every animal known to man. I've traveled from the jungles of Africa to the forests of India, working with everything from hippopotami to tarantulas.*

Q. *How strong is a gorilla compared to a man?* —D. J., RUTGERS, N.J.

A. Forget gorillas for a moment. I'll give you, for starters, just a chimpanzee. In 1924, at the Bronx zoo, a 165-pound chimpanzee recorded a right-handed pull of 847 pounds on a dynamometer. A 165-pound man's best was 210 pounds.

If that's not enough for you, a female chimpanzee at the same zoo, weighing only 135 pounds, did a pull of 1,260 pounds. The female, the record book notes, was "in a rage." Isn't that a typical chauvinistic remark? Anyway, still another chimpanzee, a male weighing only 100 pounds, managed a two-handed, dead-weight lift of 600 pounds.

Getting back to your gorilla, it's estimated a gorilla could do three times these weight-records of chimpanzees—in other words, about 2,500 pounds in a pull and, in a dead-weight lift, about 1,800 pounds. All in all, perhaps twelve times more than a person. Even one in a rage.

Q. *Do animals ever fight* for *each other?* —D. J., MARCO ISLAND, FLA.

A. Indeed they do. There are literally countless examples of animals coming to the rescue of their own species in trouble, but my favorite is the baboons. According to zoologist Philip Street, baboons are the most difficult of all animals to capture alive, not only because of their extreme cleverness in avoiding man's traps in the first place, but also because, once they are captured, they will raise such a howl that other baboons will almost surely come to their rescue.

On one occasion, Mr. Street recalls, a German animal dealer had set a trap for baboons in the traditional method of blocking access to all but one of their local watering holes, and of baiting a concealed trap at the one water source left open. When the baboons approached, the trap was sprung and the small number of baboons captured inside immediately set up bloodcurdling screams. "It must have seemed like a nightmare," Mr. Street says, in describing the counterattack of the baboons who hadn't been trapped, "as the savage hordes with bared teeth and erect manes rushed upon the hunters." Although said hunters were armed, they were no match for the angry baboons and fled precipitately, after which, he goes on, "with concentrated fury the baboons flung themselves on the trap, reducing it to a complete wreck and departing with their released fellows."

Q. *What is a hinney?* —M.G., DUMAS, TEX.

A. A badly spelled whinny. No, hinneys don't whinny, they bray—because what they are is a kind of mule, although smaller than and in some ways inferior to a mule. The mule, you see, is the offspring of a male donkey and a female horse. The hinney is the offspring of a female donkey and a male horse. Both hinneys and mules are usually sterile, but not always. A bouncing boy mule, for example, was born not long ago in Tucson, Arizona, to a mule named Maude.

Q. *Who would win in a fight between a porcupine and a skunk?* —A. T., PACIFIC GROVE, CALIF.

A. You've asked a tough question. Although both animals possess potent weapons, neither is basically a fighter and each prefers to live and let live. However, when this is impossible, both can give amazing accounts of themselves. The jet spray of liquid that the skunk emits can blind and suffocate its enemies for yards around. The porcupine has as many as thirty thousand jagged stilettos on him, and one slap of his powerful tail can drive as many as twenty of these into an enemy—enough to send a wildcat away screaming in pain. Naturalist Enos Mills once saw a fight between a porcupine and a skunk. Both, he recalled, seemed to know instinctively what a fearful weapon the other had, and both exercised, to the last possible moment, restraint. Then, almost simultaneously, they both fired. Alan Devoe has vividly recalled the end. "Porky would be smelly for a few days," he wrote, "but the skunk, his striped body riddled with any number of little barbed daggers, would have but a short time to live."

Q. *What is the difference between a panther and a puma? A cougar and a mountain lion?* —N. H., BEDFORD, OHIO

A. To all intents and purposes, none. It depends where you live. Start with the puma. South of the border (in Mexico) he's a puma. North, he's a cougar. And north of the next border (in Canada) he's a mountain lion. But all over North America the word *panther* seems to be applied to pumas, cougars and mountain lions! And just to make it really confusing, in Asia and Africa a panther is a leopard! One thing you can count on—a black panther is a black leopard everywhere.

Q. *Do any animals that are the prey of predators ever turn and prey on the predator?* —J. S., NELSONVILLE, OHIO

A. They often try, even in hopeless situations; particularly when trying to defend their young. There are many instances of animals that are always thought of as running from a fight that do the opposite in certain circumstances. A cornered kangaroo, for example, is a terrific fighter. A porcupine almost never picks a fight, but once someone has picked him—look out. He can handle a mountain lion. Even rabbits can fight—and not only well but also in extraordinarily organized fashion.

One particularly interesting predator-prey reversal is that of the owl and the crow—the difference is literally night and day. By night, sleepy crows are regularly preyed on by owls, who not only have far sharper eyes but also sharper talons and beaks. When the sun comes up, however, it's a different story. The crows are now wide awake and the owls asleep. The crows sound a rallying cry, and with many crows against one owl, it's their turn to crow and the owls turn to—well, 'owl.

Q. *What is the difference between a marmot and a marmoset?* —A.J., GARLAND, TEX.

A. A marmot is related to the squirrel and hails from North America. A small, burrowing fellow, he is brownish gray, has a short, bushy tail and is very sociable. He lives in large colonies, but each family of the colony has its own burrow and an individual member of the family to stand guard over it.

A marmoset, on the other hand, is a monkey that hails from South America. It is, as a matter of fact, the smallest monkey in the world. Indeed, the pygmy marmoset is not much bigger than a mouse. But he has long, soft fur, long, whitish ear plumes, and a ringed tail. He is, in short, beautifully odd.

Q. *You said killer whales aren't killers. I want proof.* —S. J., BOWLING GREEN, OHIO

A. I said they're not killers of man. Try this for proof: one day a couple of years ago Dr. Paul Spong, who had been working with Haida, a killer whale in the Vancouver Aquarium, was sitting on the edge of the tank with his feet in the water. Suddenly Haida came over to him, opened her incredible mouth and barely touched his feet with her teeth. The first time, Dr. Spong pulled his feet hastily out of the water in fear. But when he had put them back, and Haida kept doing it—she did it twelve times in all without leaving a scratch—Dr. Spong realized she was trying to tell him something. Dr. Spong now believes two things. The first is that killer whales may well be the only animals in the world that are not afraid of anything. And the second is that one of them, at least, tried to teach him not to be afraid of them

Q. *I've heard about the horrors of dogfights and cockfights, and even fighting fish. But come on. Is it true that* crickets *fight?* —D. S., EAST LANSING, MICH.

A. Well, since gambling has been outlawed in China, this particular "sport" has fallen on hard times—but there was a time when cricket-fighting in Asia made our World Series look like kid stuff. Indeed, there is a whole book on the subject, *Insect Musicians and Cricket Champions of China*, in which it is reported that wagers on a big-time cricket match might go as high as $100,000, and that a *shou lip*, or winning cricket, became a veritable village hero. Fed on rice, fresh cucumbers, boiled chestnuts, lotus seeds and mosquitoes, the crickets were provoked into aggressiveness by means of a bone-handled, rat-haired sort of whisk broom, which was used to goad them into action. Gray-and-black crickets were considered the best fighters, with yellow-and-grays the runners-up. But whichever strain was used, there was one sad thing in the end. The fights were to the death, and one of the crickets would, after losing an antenna, a leg and frequently having the other cricket land on his head, never go back to his hearth to chirp again.

Q. *What is the difference between a gnu and a wildebeest?* —F. B., PORTSMOUTH, N.H.

A. None—except they're both tough to pronounce. They are the same animal. Although popularly believed to belong to the ox group, they are in reality antelopes.

They are humpbacked, have buffalolike horns and horselike manes and tails. They are remarkable in that they are the fastest-running of all the antelopes—faster, for example, than even the impala—and also in that when two bulls fight, they drop to their knees first and then go at it head-on.

Although young ones are extremely playful and both old and young are gregarious with a wide variety of other animals, never underestimate the gnu, or wildebeest bull, as a fighter. He has been known to defeat a lion one to one, and in the San Francisco zoo a few months ago Toro, Jr., almost killed his keeper, Ernie Hambley. As for Toro, Sr. (Toro, Jr.,'s father), he is so fierce that he had to be placed in solitary confinement—an all-too-typical zoo solution, I am sorry to say.

Q. *Who would win in a broad-jumping contest between a man and a kangaroo?* —N. N., MILLINOCKETT, MAINE

A. The kangaroo—and by a broad margin. The broad-jump record was set by the incomparable (for a human) Bob Beamon of the United States, at the 1968 Olympic Games in Mexico. And the distance was an amazing 29 feet 2½ inches. In 1951 a red kangaroo made a series of bounds, one of which was over 42 feet.

Incidentally, man would come closer to the kangaroo in the high-jump. Champion Dwight Stones holds the world's record at 7 feet 9 inches. The kangaroo's record so far is 10 feet 6 inches. It was established naturally, too. What happened was the kangaroo was fenced in and jumped out. Then they measured the fence.

Q. *Is it true that President Kennedy himself saved the country's last mongoose?* —G. G., WEST LINN, ORE.

A. He saved one, but not the last. In 1962 a foreign sailor gave the Duluth zoo a mongoose, which, because it was nearsighted, was named Mr. Magoo. It was a big hit at the zoo, and soon was riding around on the zoo director's shoulder, just as it had on the sailor's. However—and here's the rub—the U.S. government took, if you will pardon the expression, a dim view of Mr. Magoo. It wasn't that the government had anything against Mr. Magoo personally—in fact, it doesn't have anything against any one mongoose. What it does have something against, because of the mongoose's breeding ability, is the plural of mongoose, in other words, mongeese—which, incidentally, is also wrong. It's mongooses.

You see, on the island of Jamaica, when mongooses were imported to kill snakes and rats, they not only didn't do a very good job (despite the story of Rikki Tikki Tavi, many snakes, other than the relatively slow-striking cobras, easily kill mongooses), they also soon became more of a problem than the problem. So the government, knowing the history of the immigrant mongoose in Jamaica, ordered the execution of Mr. Magoo. In vain the zoo protested that Mr. Magoo was not married; indeed there was not even a possible Mrs. Magoo within a hundred miles. They even offered to desex Mr. Magoo. But the government would have none of it. Off, they decreed, with Mr. Magoo's head. At this juncture, Secretary of the Interior Morris Udall himself intervened and ordered a stay of execution. "A classic example," President Kennedy called it, "of government by the people." In any case, the stay continued until 1968, when Mr. Magoo, still single, went by natural causes to his final reward. Today, there are a couple of dozen mongooses in zoos and research institutes. All, however, are kept under strict house rules, because the fact remains that mongooses will breed literally anywhere. If you don't believe it, there is even a story of two Egyptian mongooses who bred in a Tel Aviv zoo.

Q. *Someone told me that in a single cave in Europe they found the bones of thirty thousand bears. I don't believe it.* —T.D., WILLIAMSBURG, MICH.

A. It's true. That's what an Austrian team of archaeologists found when they excavated the so-called Dragon Cave, near Mixmitz in Styria. Or rather, that's the number of cave bears they estimated had died there, from the bones. Somewhat like our brown bear, only larger, with immense strength and a domed forehead, the cave bear, who lived during the Ice Age, was a vegetarian who bore no ill will toward man. But Ice Age man bore plenty of ill will toward him, and made him extinct. How did so many bones get in one cave? No one knows for sure, but it's assumed the bears used the caves as winter lairs, and the remains are those of bears who died there during hiberation. As someone figured, it took only one cave bear to die every third year in the cave to get that many bones.

Q. *Why is everyone so afraid of snakes?* —D.R., SPRINGDALE, ARK.

A. Why are they so afraid of mice? Actually, according to snake authority Walter Kilroy, it's usually because they have never seen a real snake close up, have never touched one or otherwise been involved with one in any way, which may be considered justification for their reaction. Most people seem to think snakes are slimy. It may be partly because snakes are cold-blooded and, therefore, not warm to the touch. The fact is that when people do summon up enough courage to touch one, they're usually nervous, and, therefore, when they make contact they do so with their palms covered with perspiration. In reality, snakes don't perspire at all and actually are a good deal less slimy than we are.

Q. *We were taking a nature walk recently and came across a frightened fawn. It just lay there, and since it didn't move my husband was sure it was hurt and wanted to take it home. At my insistence we left it there, and my husband has felt guilty ever since. What do you think we should have done?* —M.L., MILTON, MASS.

A. You did the right thing, especially in suspecting that the fawn was frightened rather than hurt. In all likelihood the mother was not far away.

If in the future you find yourself in the same situation, you could go one step further and call a local vet or conservation office and ask that the incident be investigated to find out whether the animal really is in distress.

Unless you want to support outright kidnapping of cubs, fawns and fledglings from animal mothers, or unless the animal is bleeding profusely or is in obvious physical distress, it is best to leave it where you found it and ask that the local vet or conservation officer investigate the incident, stressing that *you* are willing to take the responsibility for the animal, if it truly is in distress.

As for getting a permit to keep the animal, it is obvious that the regulations must be changed. Americans, after all, have the constitutional right to associate with whom they please. A man or woman can associate solely with animals—why cannot an animal associate solely with humans?

Why not make it more flexible to get a permit to keep the animal if you have nursed it back to health and are assured that there is no mourning mother close by. If the deer seems as contented in its new environment as it was in its natural one, why not allow it to remain as part of the family?

Should such flexibility be allowed, however, it is important that you be aware of two vital facts. First, fawns need milk or their internal organs will not develop properly. And second, male fawns develop into bucks, and they have allegedly maimed or killed many unwitting owners who have raised them from timid babies. For both reasons, you should consult an expert from the start.

Q. *You wrote recently about an animal being placed on trial in a courtroom. I understand South Africa recently tried an elephant!* —F. K., EAST ELMHURST, N.Y.

A. They did indeed. It all happened because a fellow who made friends with an elephant in Queen Elizabeth Park, outside Durban, used to go to the park very often, roll down his car window and feed the elephant. The result was that the elephant got to expect such treatment from other cars whose occupants obeyed the No Feeding, No Rolling Down Windows rules. And, of course, the inevitable happened. The elephant, after several days when his friend didn't show up, began looking for him. On several occasions he even wrapped his trunk around a car and shook it. His idea was, apparently, that nuts might fall out—but, unfortunately, not the nut that had started it all. Finally, the elephant was literally brought to trial; the charge: damage to automobiles. There were, as Gualtiero Jacopetti recalls, a judge, a public minister, a defending lawyer and even witnesses present.

The case created a furor, and this was one animal story that had a totally happy ending. The elephant was declared not guilty. By reason, presumably, of being an elephant.

NAIROBI, *Kenya:* In the middle of an African safari (camera, of course) I came upon a local booklet that asks, How well do you know your African animals? So it's my turn to question you. No stalking the answers, please. They're upside down at the end. If you get five correct, you're a tenderfoot; six, a pathfinder; seven, an assistant warden; eight, a warden; nine, an expert; and ten, me. No, I'm kidding. I'm just an assistant warden, having missed questions 2, 3 and 7.

    1. Although the cheetah is a cat, his claws are more like those of a
       (a) rat
       (b) monkey

    (c) lion

    (d) dog

2. Comparing the spots of a leopard and cheetah
   - (a) the cheetah has separate, evenly spaced spots
   - (b) the cheetah has spots in groups
   - (c) the leopard has evenly spaced spots
   - (d) both have spots in groups

3. Dik-dik deposit their droppings
   - (a) as they feed
   - (b) in a selected place they individually choose
   - (c) using a family toilet
   - (d) only near water

4. Relative to man, elephants live
   - (a) half as long
   - (b) about the same
   - (c) twice as long
   - (d) more than three times as long

5. The male gorilla will beat his chest and roar only
   - (a) after he has killed an enemy
   - (b) when he wishes to attract a mate
   - (c) when his family is threatened
   - (d) to call his family together

6. The word hippopotamus means
   - (a) water baby
   - (b) fat rump
   - (c) pot belly
   - (d) river horse

7. The mad-sounding laughter of the hyena occurs only when it is
   - (a) mating
   - (b) playing happily
   - (c) quarreling over a carcass
   - (d) warning of enemies

8. The horn of the rhinoceros is made of
   - (a) bone

(b) tough skin
(c) modified hair
(d) solid leather
9. Many grazing antelopes look alike; for example, the water-buck, puku and Uganda kob. However, they are given different and specific names because
(a) their size is different
(b) their horns are shaped differently
(c) they have different-colored markings
(d) they do not interbreed
10. Male zebra fight for dominance in the herd. Their main fighting technique is to
(a) make loud threatening noises
(b) bite each other's legs
(c) butt each other
(d) paw the ground

Advice to the Petlorn

Q. *What is the difference between a "dog person" and a "cat person"? Which are you?* —N. W., CHICAGO, ILL.

A. A dog person puts on the dog and a cat person is catty. Men like dogs, women like cats. No, seriously, I've been told there is a difference. You're a dog person if you are outgoing, make friends easily and don't demand much of friendship. You're a cat person if any of your friends now are people you disliked at first.

Which am I? Easy. I am outgoing, make friends easily and don't demand much of friendship. So—you're sure you've got it right now—I'm a cat person. The fact is, I used to be a dog person and I love and have dogs. But I've seen so many cats with so little prospect of finding homes, in pounds which they don't even call "dog and cat pounds," but just dog pounds, that, well, I think they need all the help they can get.

Q. *My boyfriend loves cats. I love dogs. He says that writer Albert Payson Terhune said that cats are smarter. Tell him he's wrong!* —N. H., BUDDEFORD, MAINE

A. If you think I'm going to get into that argument—no way. But your boyfriend is right. Albert Payson Terhune felt cats were smarter. He based this on the fact that whenever a dog was thirsty he would wait by the faucet until someone turned it on. A cat, on the other hand, would try to figure it out and turn the tap on itself.

Q. *Why do you think that more women seem to prefer cats as pets, and more men seem to prefer dogs?* —C. G., MILLEDGEVILLE, GA.

A. Based on my own private poll, a lot of women like cats because they identify with, or at least strongly appreciate, the cat's independence and self-possession. On the other hand, men like the image of the devoted dog curled at their feet—the faithful companion who would follow them unquestioningly, anywhere. Add to this the general female preference for the fastidiousness and cleanliness of the cat, versus the general male preference for the casual do-as-you-pleaseness of the dog. All this does not mean that I do not recognize the hordes of female dog-lovers and male cat-lovers, but these women are perhaps less—well, feline—and the men less—well, dogged. I think I'll quit here before I offend everybody.

Q. *Is it true cats are smarter crossing streets than dogs?* —A. T., DANBURY, CONN.

A. One thing is certain—they're faster. And some are smarter.

If you don't believe it, ask a friend of mine, Cyril Moore, an assistant attorney general in New York and a true animal man (he has everything from dogs and cats to a yak). Anyway, Mr. Moore lives in Litchfield, Connecticut, and for the last three years a cat named Pleasure Unit (don't you love the name?) owned by William Armstrong, who wrote *Sounder*, used to commute three miles to Mr. Moore's place to catch a dinner.

Pleasure Unit went over steep, sometimes icy, traffic-clogged roads and never was injured. "He literally stopped before he crossed the street and looked both ways," says Mr. Moore, who saw him do it many times.

The story has a sad ending. Pleasure Unit wanted all his life to be a house cat, and when he finally made it and the Moores tried to keep down his wandering, he followed a friend outside, came to the road and, now careless, didn't look both ways. He was killed.

Q. *Why do people talk so sneeringly about "cat people"?* —E. S., BRANDENBERG, KY.

A. People talk that way about those who rescue and take in, in many cases, more cats than they can properly handle. Such people shouldn't be sneered at—it is not a crime to have a bigger heart than head. They should, wherever possible, be assisted. People who love cats may well be the truest of all animal people; they love the animal for the animal's sake, not for their own sakes—for their beauty, for their grace of movement, even for their very independence. Incidentally, one cat person, Rosanne Amberson, in her book *Raising Your Cat* tells a fascinating story about convicts nearing their release dates who were allowed to have cats in their cells. Of the men who loved and cared for their cats, not a single one later failed as a free man to adjust to society. Dog people please note—cats were chosen only because they were easier to care for and not necessarily because the experiment wouldn't have worked with them, too.

Q. *Are dogs and cats right- or left-pawed, like humans are?*
—T. C., ALBUQUERQUE, N.M.

A. Many people have claimed that their animals are either right- or left-pawed by the fact they favor one for doing certain things. However, I've never believed it, and my lack of paw prejudice is backed up by none other than Dr. William Kay of New York's Animal Medical Center—who, as a clinical neurologist, has been involved in much research on the subject. "I've searched the evidence for answers to the question," he told me, "and I can find none that indicates there is a dominance of one side of the brain over the other, which would in turn indicate that the animal would prefer his right paw to left or vice versa."

Q. *Cats seem to me to be, generally speaking, worse-tempered than dogs. Am I wrong?* —A. J., KENYON, OHIO

A. Yes. Cats are not worse-tempered than dogs. They are smaller and have a harder time both defending themselves and fending for themselves. But, generally speaking, they are only bad-tempered when they have been given good reason to be—which is more than you can say for most humans.

Q. *My cat watches TV, but my dog pays no attention to it. Why?*
—P. L., DAYTON, O.

A. Your dog is a critic. Seriously, columnist Harriet Van
Horne, who used to write television criticism, has a Persian named
Poof who really was in her own way a critic. She liked animal
shows but was so dissatisfied with other TV fare she used to stand
in front of the set and scrub at it with her paws. She wasn't just
trying to clean it up, either. Ms. Van Horne swears that once Poof
audibly purred, "Out, damned spot!" Actually what animal
TViewers like is the movement and the sounds—particularly animal sounds.

And there is no question that for every dog fan there are at
least a dozen cat fans. Out in Boulder, Colorado, for example,
there's a cat named Tiz who "discovered" TV the night they put
on *Bird Man of Alcatraz*. Since then, her favorite program has been
"Lassie," which she likes to watch from the top of the set, patting
or bashing the hero—her family isn't quite sure which. In New

York, a young lady named Rosanna who works at Celebrity Service has a Great Dane who, she claims, favors Westerns. "When a man is shot or knocked down," she declares, "he will look for him under the set." Finally, at the Dallas zoo there's a parrot named Charlene. She not only likes TV, she's a part of it. Her favorites are soap operas; she picks up names and phrases and talks right back at them.

Q. *I want to have both a cat and a dog. My father says I can have only one or the other because they are natural enemies.* —C. G., GAMBIER, OHIO

A. Your father is wrong. Despite the expression, Fighting like cats and dogs, cats and dogs are not natural enemies. Unfortunately, they are not natural friends, either. Because of size, for one reason, the cat is afraid of the dog. And because of this, the cat either assumes the defensive attitude or turns tail and flees. The former response arouses the dog's fighting instinct, while the latter incites his urge to give chase. Either action by the dog is likely to place the cat in trouble, particularly if it has been declawed and cannot fight back or climb out of danger.

Still, you can have both of them if you get them both as youngsters. Then you are home free from the beginning. If you already have an older cat, introduce it to a young puppy; if you have an old dog, bring home a young kitten. Here, you are not quite home free—a sharp watch and special attention given to the older dog or cat is necessary. Don't make him or her feel unwanted because of the new arrival.

The most difficult situation is when you introduce a grown-up dog to a grown-up cat—or vice versa—especially in a house where one has been king of the castle.

Here the proper way to do it is to keep the newcomer in a separate room for several days, primarily so they can get used to the smell of each other. And it's absolutely essential that you give the old-timer extra-special attention and affection.

Q. *Where does the word* pedigree *actually come from?* —J. Z., MEADOWBROOK, PA.

A. It comes from the French phrase *pied de grue* and it means "foot of a crane." Why a crane? Well, in the old days, the three-line graph of lineal descent used in the documents recording a family tree looked just like a crane's foot. What does a crane's foot look like? Easy. Like a pedigree. That should give pause to anyone who's snobbish about the word—or the fact.

Q. *Is it true that long-haired cats have more sense than short-haired cats?* —T. P., SALEM, OHIO

A. Yes, just like short-haired people (in the old days, men) have more sense than long-haired people (i.e., women). Seriously, the answer is no. Many people really do believe, however, that long-haired cats are less independent than short-haired ones. I've still got to be shown, though, and I'd be interested in any documentation from any reader.

Q. *What's so great about Siamese cats? They aren't my favorites.* —Y. R., DERBY, CONN.

A. They aren't a lot of people's—but they also *are* a lot of people's. That's the great thing about people and pets. It takes all kinds—of both. The other day a man in New York, Frank Glynn, sent me a picture of his Siamese, and with it was a letter—one that I'd like to share with you:

> *How nutty can you get about a cat you got for nothing? This scrawny-looking Siamese was wished upon us by our daughter. I, a cat man, can't resist cats, especially alley cats. Whatever they are, alley or pedigree, they are my kind of animal—housewise. As smart as I think I am, I know that they are smarter than I am—but I would never tell that to any cat. Perhaps they know that but they are so condescending that they let me believe that I am a superior person in the cat family and that as long as I behave properly they will tolerate me, even though I wear trousers, which they consider as ladders.*
>
> *No one should live alone. Get a cat, any cat. Fix up a litter box in the bathroom, a water dish, a simple toy (a rolled-up cigarette*

package or Ping-Pong ball) and you will have a friend who will never let you get into the doldrums, especially if you have a soft comforter on the bed.

So much more could I say.

Q. *What breed of dog has the longest record of popularity? What are the five most popular breeds?* —A. O'T., BENWOOD, W. VA.

A. Mutts—by a mile. It's just like I've always said about humans—you know, a good family is one that used to be better. Show me a purebred and what have you got? A show dog. But show me a mutt and you've got it all—the world by the tail. Actually, the purebred dog who'd win the race with the longest record of popularity is the beagle. And that, too, seems to bear out my mutt theory, because the little guy seems to me to be the closest to an all-breed.

According to AKC records, the poodle is still the most popular, but he's definitely slipping, and the German shepherd, obviously for his protection value, is gaining fast. But the beagle stays right up there year after year in the number two or number three spot. Second to the beagle, and even gaining on him, is a little guy I bet you never would have guessed: the dachshund. Finally, coming on fast is a fellow I'm sure no one would have guessed. He was twenty-sixth in popularity only ten years ago, and he's now fifth. Sure 'n' he's none other than your wild Irish setter. The larger breeds have grown more popular, undoubtedly due to the protection inducement. Ten years ago, for example, chihuahuas, Pekingese and Pomeranians were all on the "Ten Most" list. So, among the medium-sized dogs, was the basset. Now, among the medium-sized dogs, only the beagle, dachshund and cocker spaniel have held their positions. Among the big dogs, the two that gained most besides the Irish setter were the Doberman pinscher (now sixth, he was twenty-second) and the Saint Bernard (now tenth, he was twenty-fourth).

Q. *How did the Manx cat get its name? Why don't they have tails?*
—J. E., RIPLEY, MISS.

A. They come from the Isle of Man, between England and Ireland, where the people, too, are called Manx. According to legend, the cats lost their tails when Noah slammed the door of the ark. Actually, a few years ago the Isle's cats were fast becoming an endangered species, due to visiting cat rustlers. Now they're protected and there's a government-operated cattery which produces about forty kittens a year. They'll cost you only eighteen dollars, but freight to the United States is sixty-two dollars. The reason there are so few of them is, according to Isle historian Arthur Griffiths, that in almost every litter there are rejects—cats born with "appendages." I don't like the sound of it. Try your local shelter.

Q. *Everybody always says, a grin like a Cheshire cat. I want to know (a) are there Cheshire cats, (b) do they grin?* —M.B., CARTERSVILLE, GA.

A. There is no special breed of cat known as the Cheshire. But when Lewis Carroll, in *Alice's Adventures in Wonderland*, had the grinning cat gradually disappear from Alice's view, he used a legend that goes 'way back. The famous dictionary editor, Charles Evans Funk, noted that because Cheshire was a place in England that had regal privileges, the cats were so happy to be there they couldn't help grinning. He also notes, however, the more likely

story that some influential Cheshire families who had coats of arms which included a happy lion had painters who were not too sure of what a lion looked like, and so went along with a happy cat.

Q. *What kind of cat do you think is the prettiest?* —H. G., BILLINGS, MONT.

A. Yours.

Q. *Have you ever heard of a breed of dog called a* mud hound? *I've heard they can exist in the desert because wherever they are, they can find water.* —U. M., SAN FRANCISCO, CALIF.

A. For years I have heard of such a dog—one who's not just a Bowser the Hound, but a kind of Dowser the Hound. Frankly, I never believed it. Not long ago, however, I met a young man named Steve Stein, the producer of a radio program in Chicago. He was given a pup mud hound by a girlfriend, and he's had the dog, named Dusty, for two and a half years. He loves Dusty, who is brown and white and who has a very distinctive brown ring around his right eye. Mr. Stein's girlfriend told him that mud hounds were bred by the Mississippi Valley Indians and that there were only about thirty of them—at least of purebreds—left in this country. The woman also told him that they were used by the early settlers to cross the desert. The settlers' wagons had to carry a large amount of water, and yet the more they carried, the longer it took them to reach the next place where they could get it. So, she told him, they took mud hounds, who liked to roll around in the mud so much that they went out to find mud, and that led anybody who followed them to an area where there was water. One wagon train, however, ran out of water, and the people who went out after the dogs couldn't keep up with them. They died of thirst but the dogs came back, and from then on the dogs have had a bad reputation. Mr. Stein told the woman, "Oh, sure." He liked Dusty so much, he didn't care whether the story was true. Not long ago, however, he moved to a small town in Illinois named Makanda. And one evening, when he was rapping with some old friends, they saw his dog and said: "That must be one of those mud hounds." Whereupon they told him the exact same story about the wagon train. Now Mr. Stein isn't so sure about his "Oh, sure."

Q. *Why is a cocker spaniel called a "cocker"?* —L. G., CHARLOTTESVILLE, VA.

A. Because in the old days he hunted woodcock. Then one day, deep in the woods, he came upon a little woodcock face-to-face. He put down his gun—excuse me—he never hunted again.

Q. *Once a reader asked you, "Is there any dog that doesn't bark?" and you replied in the negative. I am enclosing a pamphlet describing such a dog.* —W. R. W., STILL RIVER, MASS.

A. I didn't. I myself have two dogs, Siberian huskies, who almost never bark. But I'll take your bum rap anyway, because your pamphlet on the basenji is so intriguing. In fact, I'd like to quote from it:

> *An endearing, fascinating little fellow, full of play yet gentle as a kitten. His fastidious habits, such as cleaning himself as does a cat, his lack of doggy odors, make him an ideal dog for the immaculate housekeeper. The basenji adores his owners, loves children and is tireless in play. The quietness of the basenji is not without voice. His growl of warning is serious sounding and would frighten off any marauder. And his yodel of happiness thrills those who love him.*

Q. *I want to know how to pronounce Shih Tzu, and also whether Shih Tzus and Lhasa apsos are the same dog.* —A. H., FALLSTON, MD.

A. Absolutely not. In fact, up until 1950, the American Kennel Club registered the Shih Tzu as a Lhasa, and it was not until 1969 that the Shih Tzu was granted full recognition.

The Peking Kennel Club once issued a "standard" for the Shih/Lhasa which the *International Encyclopedia of Dogs* called "the most flowery every issued for any breed." I won't dispute this. "The Lhasa Dog," it said, "should have lion head, bear torso, camel hoof, feather-duster tail, palm-leaf ears, rice teeth, pearly petaled tongue and movement like a goldfish."

Don't worry about its pronunciation—actually it's pronounced *Shid Zoo*—just worry about how to housebreak it. On that score, Shih Tzus are holy terrors, as befitting the fact that they and the Lhasas are the holy dogs of the East. In the immortal words of a friend of mine, Mrs. Bernard Seligman of New York: "Shih Tzus are very clean dogs. Whenever they wet in the house, they never walk in it."

Mrs. Seligman may joke about her two Shih Tzus, but the fact is although she and her husband have had Boston terriers, boxers and poodles, there is no question that they regard their Shih Tzus as something else again.

"They're both playful dogs and yet also restful dogs," Mrs. Seligman told me. "They adore fun, but they're incredibly sensitive. When one of the kids is sick, I know it right away from the greeting I get from the dogs at the door. They literally can't wait to march me into the kids' rooms.

"They are so bright, too. I don't just talk to them, they talk to me. And both of them have such totally different personalities. One is like a wound-up toy, the other is like a Garbo cat."

Mrs. Seligman warns only about two things. One is that Shih Tzus are not protective dogs. "They are too small," she says, "and they are smart enough to know it." The other is that they are not hot-weather dogs. "They actually get sick from heat," she says, "and literally crazed from humidity. They've got to have air conditioning."

Q. *What is the most valuable dog?* —C. D., YOUNGSTOWN, OHIO

A. Yours—and if you have the right relationship with him, no amount of money could ever pay for him. But if you mean the rarest, the rarest dog in the world today is the Lowchen, which is Chinese for lion dog. During the Renaissance he was very popular and the lapdog of half the nobility of southern Europe. But at last count there were only fifty-two in the world: forty-five on British laps, five on West German laps and two on Mallorcan laps.

Q. *You wrote about that English sheepdog and how affectionate he was. I don't agree about another shaggy, eyeless wonder—the Lhasa apso. A friend of mine has one, and every time we visit, he barks furiously and acts as if we were total strangers.* —F. P., AZTEC, N. MEX.

A. Lhasas are known to be extremely chary of strangers. In fact, most of them are inclined to greet all visitors with none-too-friendly sounding barks. For one thing, they have a very strong sense of guardianship. For another, they are extremely loyal to their owners, and rarely can be enticed, even by food or other bribery methods, to divide this loyalty. Indeed, if owned by a male, they are inclined to take a dim view of most females—and vice versa. Why? Well, maybe it's all that hair. After all, they really do have a dim view.

Q. *I hear dog people talking about cock-a-poos and peek-a-boos. Are they real breeds?* —R. L., COLD SPRING HARBOR, N.Y.

A. Well, they're not recognized by the AKC, but the fact is you can mix almost anything. And some mixtures make wonderful dogs, even if their names sound like something you don't like on the sidewalk. A cock-a-poo is a mixture of cocker and poodle. Your "peek-a-boo" is, in reality, a peek-a-*poo*—again a poodle, but this time mixed with a Pekingese. Loretta Swit, of "M*A*S*H" fame, now starring on Broadway in *Same Time, Next Year*, is particularly big on peek-a-poos; she has two of them. "They're *beautiful*," she assured me. "They look like a throw pillow and you've really got the best of both breeds. I love the independence of the Pekingese, but their shedding can drive you crazy. The peek-a-poo doesn't shed, and he's a very bright dog. They're not as yappy and high-strung as a poodle. They've got it together; they don't come apart." Ms. Swit smiled. "After all," she said, "you've got the French and the Chinese—the naughty and the inscrutable. What more can you ask?"

Q. *What do you think of those fancy poodle cuts?* —M. B., KINGS-TON, TENN.

A. I think they're awful. They look like sheep who've been halfway through a sheep dip. I never saw a show poodle yet who wouldn't look better with a plain bear cut. Then there's also the matter of the Dutch or sport cut—which is a bare back and fluff on the shoulders and backside. They look like they just came out of a bad barber school.

Q. *Why are Yorkshire terriers so aggressive?* —M. K., PINE PLAINS, N.Y.

A. You would be, too, if you were that little and had all that hair in front of your face and had something fifty times your size and weight telling you what to do all the time. Yorkies are, in-cidentally, a man-made breed, being a composite of several terriers, including something called a broken-haired Scottish terrier, a

Clydesdale or Paisley terrier, a Skye terrier, a black-and-tan (now known as a Manchester terrier) and, 'way back in the days of King William IV, a waterside terrier. Yorkshire terriers first became a recognized breed, spunkiness and all, in 1840—the result of a mating between a female called Old Kitty and a male named Old Crab. No, I *didn't* make it up!

Q. *Are Saint Bernards still used to rescue people? How do they do it?*
—J. A., WALDRON, IND.

A. Yes, they are still there, at the famous Hospice du Grand Saint Bernard in the Swiss Alps, albeit nowadays helicopters have made them primarily picturesque. Saint Bernards were first used to lead people over trails buried in snow and, in doing this, demonstrated such a remarkable ability to smell that they literally sniffed out their first jobs—people who had fallen under the snow. A large number of men in Napoleon's army were saved by Saint Bernards and, more recently, the famous Barry in twelve years rescued no less than forty persons. Ironically, he was killed by the forty-first—an idiot who thought it was a bear coming at him and killed him with an ice axe. Ironically, too, Saint Bernards rarely carried around their necks the kegs so loved by cartoonists. One did, though. He went out with a large sign on his keg marked Whiskey, faithfully followed by a puppy. The puppy's keg was marked Chaser. There is no truth, however, to the story that a third dog sallied forth with a keg marked Very Dry.

Q. *I feel so strongly about those awful-named dogs, those wolfhounds, elkhounds, deerhounds, otterhounds, bloodhounds and even boarhounds, that now I'm against fox terriers and pointers and setters. But have you ever heard of a* lionhound? *Do they really hunt lions?* —W. L., OVERLEA, MD.

A. It's not a lionhound—it's a lion dog. What it actually is, is a Rhodesian ridgeback, or, as it's more formally called, the Rhodesian ridgeback lion dog. Unlike the Chinese lion dog, it's a big, powerful dog that didn't originally come from Rhodesia, but from South Africa. But don't be too hard on these ridgebacks, who are particularly good-natured, dependable and excellent with children, or, for that matter, on *any* of those hounds you mentioned. In the first place, with a few cruel exceptions, such as otterhounds, they don't hunt their namesakes anyway. And, in the second place, they are all remarkable dogs. The Norwegian elkhound, as I've said before, is one of the most intelligent of all dogs. In a book on the breed by Helen Franciose and Nancy Swanson, the story is told of a female elkhound who could get out of any fenced enclosure as long as there were other dogs enclosed. One day her owner watched in amazement as the elkhound first rounded up the other dogs in perfect order, like steps close to the fence, then took a run at the steps and leaped over.

Q. *Why do people who breed dogs get to look so much like them?*
—J. D., ROXBURY, CONN.

A. It's funny—and there is also some truth to it, as you can prove for yourself at any dog show. It's always a fascinating speculation. On one occasion, for example, I spoke at a federation of dog clubs' meeting and I swear I could tell, say, the collie table from the sheepdog table just by the hair, and the schnauzer table from the bulldog table by the jowls. But a recent survey on the subject made among a large number of dog owners didn't bear this out.

What the survey did bear out, however, according to author Farley Manning, was that people are inclined to own the kind of dog that reflects their own personalities. Add to this the fashions, like a woman with a poodle-cut or a young man on campus who looks like a Lhasa apso, and you get the picture that results in the movie star who looks like a collie, the model who looks like an Afghan, the comedian who looks like a basset and the society matron and spouse who look—although we're not saying which is which—like a Pekingese and a pug. What kind of dogs are my favorites? Hey, wait a minute, my favorites are mutts.

Q. *It seems to me that many dogs and cats are overbred, I guess for dog- and cat-show purposes. Anyway, some can't even function the way they were originally supposed to. How do you feel about this?* —P. M., DE RIDDER, LA.

A. I think it's bad, as you obviously do. The short-nosed dogs, for example—the boxers, pugs, Pekes, and so on—have a hard time, particularly in summertime, just breathing. Persian cats suffer in summer, too—from those enormous coats. As for Siamese, some are so cross-eyed they can't even see properly.

And it isn't just dogs and cats, either. Take goldfish. There is, for example, a goldfish called the *celestial* that is very much prized—in fact they can cost one hundred dollars apiece—but over generations, they have been bred to see in the strangest way possible—indeed, in one sense, they can't see at all—they have curiously telescoped eyes and can only see upward. In other words, if they were not protected as pets, they'd be totally helpless. They can't see either what's ahead of them or what might be coming after them.

Then there's another kind of goldfish called the *lionhead*. They not only look very odd (they look as though they have a disease all over their heads) but also their fins have been so reduced, again by generations of "selective breeding," that they can't even swim properly. When you get to breeding fish that can't swim, it seems to me it's time for a purebred to marry a peasant.

Q. *Why is it that people go to shelters and demand a purebred? Didn't you say mutts were better pets?* —G. M., EAST CHICAGO, ILL.

A. Yes I did, and I stick to it. For affectionateness and good temperament and—well, not being overbred—you can't beat the all-around, deep-down goodness you get from that all-American dog who's everything. My favorite story on this subject is about the woman in New York who has a shelter and came across the least prepossessing dog you ever saw: a timid fellow who looked like a cross between a big beagle and a bad borzoi. And who do you think adopted it? A Park Avenue snob who demanded a purebred.

Here's how it happened. The daughter of the Park Avenuer, who shall be nameless, fell in love with the scruffy fellow at the shelter. "Why don't you get him?" my friend at the shelter asked her. "Oh," she said, "I couldn't. My father wouldn't let a mutt into the apartment." My friend didn't bat an eyelash. "A mutt!" she exclaimed. "Why, this dog is one of the rarest breeds in the world." "What breed?" the daughter wanted to know. My friend, looking at the dog, thought quickly. "He is," she said slowly, "a Portuguese palace dog." It was the daughter's turn to look at the dog. "I've never heard of that breed," she said, doubtfully. My friend warmed to her task. "There's no reason why you should have," she said. "They're so rare. Only one is allowed to be exported every four years." The girl was happier now. "But why is he so timid? He doesn't like people." My friend decided to go all out. "Oh, that," she said. "That's because he isn't used to associating with anyone but royalty."

The story goes on, but the long and short of it (and the dog is both) is that the Park Avenue snob is now so delighted with his daughter's "rare breed" that he even took it down to the bank where he works to show it off and tell about it. The only thing he's bothered about is why his daughter didn't obtain any papers when she got the dog. The daughter called my friend. "Oh," she said, "dogs like that don't have pedigrees. They have coats of arms." She's now working on drawing one up.

Q. *If you could only have one kind of dog for the rest of your life, what kind would it be? Why?* —O. L., KENNETT SQUARE, PA.

A. A mutt shepherd. I think they have the highest intelligence combined with the most highly developed sense of responsibility and affection.

Q. *Why are guinea pigs called guinea pigs?* —W. C., DANBY, VT.

A. They shouldn't be, and I want you to stop it right away. In the first place, they are not pigs, they are members of the rodent family. And in the second place, they don't come from Guinea or even New Guinea. They were introduced to Europe by the Dutch, who got them from their colonies on the Guiana coast of South America. There are three distinct forms of guinea pigs: the English, or crew-cut, variety; the Peruvian, or hippie-hair, variety; and the Abyssinian, or beauty-parlor variety. Among guinea pig myths is that they breed tremendously rapidly; but they don't. They are slow reproducers and, indeed, it often takes three months for an adult pair even to get to know each other. Their litters are also quite small—three, on the average. They make excellent pets—inquisitive, charming and fun—if handled with concern, given the proper diet and water and approached with friendship. Indeed, they make ideal apartment pets for people who, because of stupid rules, can't have dogs or cats.

Q. *What is the difference between a gerbil and a hamster? Which is a better pet for my kids?* —J. G., POLK, PA.

A. I am going to go along with the gerbil, even though it's not as pretty. Both are members of the rodent family but, let's face it, a gerbil *looks* more like a rat. But the fact remains it sleeps at night—not, as the hamster does, in the daytime—and this alone makes it a more satisfactory pet. However, there are disadvantages to the gerbil. In some states, notably California, they are illegal, the idea being they will get loose, breed and destroy crops. This is unfortunate because, between the two, there is no question that gerbils have better dispositions. The only qualities they don't have, compared to hamsters, are looks and fascination. Here hamsters are supreme.

A golden hamster is really a beautiful little animal, and its pouch, in which it can store an incredible amount of food, is an unending source of fascination for small fry. Please don't think, when your hamster has some food in there, that he's got the mumps. One particular beef I have with pet stores about both these animals is that they either won't or don't bother to find out what sex they are. It's difficult—but it can be done. Another is that too many of the pet-care books do not put enough emphasis on the danger of these pets falling. Since they have poor vision and no instinctive fear of heights, they can easily fall out of your hand or off the table. Then, since they are not, like cats and squirrels, able to turn their bodies in midair, they can suffer terrible injuries.

Q. *My brother says guinea pigs make better pets than rabbits. I say rabbits do. Who's right?* —M. T., SILVER BAY, MINN.

A. Why doesn't your brother get a guinea pig, and you get a rabbit? They will get along fine together, and maybe one of these days you and your brother will, too. Seriously, rabbits and guinea pigs eat essentially the same food: rabbit pellets, fresh vegetables, and so on (but don't feed your rabbit cabbage, and give your guinea pig plenty of Vitamin C). And if guinea pigs are, perhaps, easier pets, since they are smaller and can be comfortably contained in a small (but not too small) cage, rabbits have the advantage that they can be housebroken to a litter box. Guinea pigs can't.

Q. *My neighbor has offered me a couple of rabbits for pets, and I'd love to have them. However, neither my neighbor nor I can tell whether they are males or females. I don't want to keep just one and have it be lonely, and I don't want a litter on my hands. What should I do?* —M. H., WALNUT CREEK, CALIF.

A. Trundle the two off to your vet, and let him tell you which is which. You probably won't want to keep two males—they may fight. If yours are a mixed pair, why not have the male neutered? That way, the three of you can live happily ever after without the problem of the patter of tiny new paws every few weeks. Remember, rabbits breed like rabbits.

Q. *Why don't you write something about turtles—especially about painting them?* —H. C., MATTAPOISETT, MAINE

A. I'd love to. Painting turtles is horrible—it deforms their shells, disorganizes their body functions and condemns them to ever-increasing pain and, finally, brutal death. I'm glad to report, though, that interest in turtles is growing by leaps and bounds. If you don't believe it, take the story of New York's Martha Reeves, who's writing a book about turtles. "One day," she told me, "I ran into a fellow author, Madeleine L'Engle—she wrote *The Total Turtle*, you know—and she told me to go to a pet shop at Broadway and 106th Street and buy two turtles they had there. I'd never had any turtles, but I didn't ask any questions. I presumed they were turtles in trouble. Anyway, I bought them and when I got home I put them in a brandy snifter. I built a ceramic bridge in it and one day I saw one of the turtles climbing out of the water onto the bridge.

"Something snapped in me. I realized I'd never really looked at a turtle before. Suddenly he was like the first creature crawling out of some primeval lost lagoon. And suddenly I wanted to know all about him, everything—where he came from, and especially how to take care of him. I'd always heard that in New York you could form a society for anything and get a hundred members. So I started one, and do you know how many members the New York Turtle and Tortoise Society has now?" We shook our head. "Two hundred," she said. How many turtles, we asked, did she now have? "I only have twenty-five," she said, "but last summer, when I had a lot of boarders, I was up to eighty. And I'm not counting," she concluded quietly, "tortoises or iguanas."

Q. We just got two red-eared turtles for our classroom. Their names are Happy and Tappy. We would like to know how we can tell if they are boys or girls. —GUY DRUMMOND SCHOOL, GRADE 1, ROOM 3.

A. You've got me—or, rather, you had me until I went to authority Joe Davis. He advises me that if the turtle's undershell is slightly more concave—in other words, if it bulges in—he's a male. Also that the vent on the male is farther out on the tail. Meanwhile, while on the subject of turtles, don't believe all the hysteria these days about turtle diseases. All known turtle diseases transferable to man can be effectively dealt with by one simple precaution: after you've played with your turtle, wash your hands thoroughly.

Q. *My turtles won't eat. What do I do?* —N. F., NORWALK, CONN.

A. Most people don't realize that the popular pet store turtles—usually red-eared sliders—are aquatic turtles and need water. Ideally, they should live in an aquarium with at least six inches of water and a rack or ledge so that they can climb out to dry. Aquatic turtles even eat underwater. According to turtle expert Donna West, many commercial turtle foods are not adequate, and you should at least add to them a mixture of meat, fish and fresh greens. Turtles also like bits of tomatoes and bananas. Above all, don't put aquatic turtles in shallow, plastic turtle bowls, as some people do, and just sprinkle in something like dried shrimp every day. This is sure, slow death for the turtle.

Q. *I promised my grandson an aquarium for his birthday. He seems to have his heart set on a kind of Marineland in his own house. I go back to the days of goldfish bowls. What am I getting into, anyway?* —P. L., NAPLES, FLA.

A. In the first place, goldfish bowls are out—they are hard to clean, for one thing, but more important, they give a distorted view of the inside. Rectangular tanks are the thing today. It will cost you about sixty dollars to give your grandson a good start: fifteen dollars or so for a good ten-gallon tank, fifteen dollars more for a good filtering system (don't stint here) and seven dollars or so for a thermostatic heating system (goldfish can live in cold water, but the kind of fish he will want—tropical fish—need a temperature of seventy-five to eighty degrees). His lighting system (again, don't stint) will run you sixteen dollars. All right, throw in four dollars for plant life and you've got eight dollars left for fish. Don't despair. Fish go as high as three hundred dollars each, but they also go as low as thirty-five cents each, and some of my favorites, like silver tips or head-and-taillights, are just eighty-five cents per.

The important thing is to get "community" fish—fish who like each other. Otherwise you'll have an unhappy aquarium. Consult your local fish market—excuse me, your pet fish man—and follow his advice. José Morales, who's been in the business for many years, tells me to warn your grandson about tiger barbs. They're very colorful—black and gold—but they fight; particularly if there are only two. "If you have six or more, they won't fight," he says, "as much." Consider yourself warned. As for telling the difference between boy fish and girl fish, lots of luck. It can be done—but not by many.

Q. *How many times a day should I feed my fish?* —O. A., TRACY, CALIF.

A. Well, let's say they don't need breakfast, lunch and dinner. But you'd better go back to your local tropical fish store, or aquarium, and find out what's best for the particular kind of fish you have. Certain kinds of tropical fish do have to eat at least twice a day, and some kinds cannot survive long on one feeding. Most fish, in other words, like most people, are better off with more small meals and fewer big meals. Overfeeding fish, just like overwatering plants, is one of the most common causes of real trouble.

Q. *You get my goat—because you never write anything* about *goats. They're wonderful animals and they make marvelous pets.* —C. M., SHARON, PA.

A. *Touché!* I should have. And you're right. But before I get started about how great they are, let me ask you a question. Where did that expression, Get my goat, come from? Not even from a goat; it came from the goatee. Dictionary editor Charles Funk proved the expression was never in print before 1912, the high point of the era of the goatee. Anyway, one couple I know, Bob and Linda Hale of Wellesley, Massachusetts, have no less than twenty goats. "People are so sensitive about goats," Mrs. Hale told me. "They do not smell and they do not eat tin cans. In fact, they are fastidious eaters, and if anything drops to the ground, they won't eat it. The only thing goats really are is sexy. That I can't argue!" Mrs. Hale paused. "But that's it," she continued. "They are intelligent, curious and very responsive. They love to be patted. Compared to ponies—and we also have ponies—goats are much more sociable. They don't need another goat, but they do need another loyal friend. And they make wonderful friends, even of nervous racehorses." We thought Mrs. Hale was through, but she wasn't. "And don't call the females *nannies*," she concluded. "They are *does*. They are marvelous mothers—so protective of their young." The Hales particularly love pygmy goats, which they raise. "When I take them in the car," Mrs. Hale said, "they never make a mistake. A friend of mine has one of ours, and it comes in at tea-time and sits on a chair just like a person."

Q. *Can you really tell the age of a horse from its teeth?* —C. V., CINCINNATI, OHIO

A. Yes. A horse's permanent teeth—those in the center of his jaw—come in when he's two and a half years old. At three and a

half, another set of teeth, beside the first, comes in, and at four and a half a third set appears. After that, you have to judge by the age of the teeth, and thus it's tougher. Tougher to—well, look a gift-horse in the mouth. But you can still get your information straight from the horse's mouth. How about that—I got both of them in.

Q. *Why are gray horses supposed to be unlucky?* —M. G., MINDEN, LA.

A. They aren't—and if you repeat that silly superstition, you'll grow warts. Actually, just to show you how silly it really is, there are some horsey circles where a gray horse is thought to bring not bad luck but good. In the show ring, for example, there is a firm belief among equestrians that a gray horse is more likely to get a favorable rating than a nongray, because his unusual color will more closely attract the judge's eye. And in medieval tournaments, while the good guy supposedly rode a white horse, quite often, according to horsewoman Jane Poulton, it tended toward the gray side. A horse's color, of course, has absolutely nothing to do with its speed, strength, stamina, temperament or personality. And, despite what race track buffs may tell you, dapple grays have even had an enviable record on the turf—as witness the peerless Native Dancer. As for me, I don't horse around. I think they are all—bays, blacks, roans, sorrels and grays—you guessed it—great.

Q. *Settle an argument, please. Are there more or less horses around than in the old days?* —G. S., MILWAUKEE, WIS.

A. Far less for work, far more as, well, pets. There were two million horses in this country in 1960 and there are nine million today. After all, if bikes are back, can horses be far behind?

Q. *Is it true horses are dumb?* —W. W., MIAMI, FLA.

A. If you mean that with rare exceptions, such as "Mr. Ed," they can't talk—yes. If you mean are they unintelligent—well, here is a letter from a young lady, Louise Stange of Englewood, Ohio, who knows more about horses than you or I will ever learn.

> *Those people who say horses aren't intelligent are showing their own ignorance. They have not been around horses nor understand them. I have been close to horses for sixteen years, and know for a fact that they each possess their own distinct personalities. Personal experience has shown that they are extremely bright and intuitive. My two half-Arabians, Marti and Sunni, have been close friends and companions for twelve years. Sunni is Marti's daughter, and she's been with me from the day she was born. When she was just three years old, we were riding in a field arena. I did not see the other horses in the corner by some trees. One horse had a reputation for being foul-tempered. The horse came up and kicked me in the leg. The jolt threw me out of the saddle and onto the ground. Sunni took over from there. She bent her head down and checked on me, then ran over and dispatched a few well-placed kicks on the attacker. She then rushed right back over to return to me. She stood over me and dared the offender to try again.*
>
> *Sunni's mother, Marti, in addition to getting into everything to investigate, has acquired an unusual talent. When four years old, she discovered that by flapping her lips, she obtained an excessive amount of attention and found this was one way of making her needs known. She holds her lips limp, then shakes her head, letting her lips flap up and down. All I have to do is ask her to "flap your lips," no matter where it may be, and she will obligingly give it her all. A local television station even sent out a cameraman to film her in action for their six o'clock newsreel. Of course, she had to examine the camera!*
>
> *Whenever I walk into the barn, or into the field, all I have to do is call, and Sunni and Marti are at my side. They each have their own ways of saying hello. Sunni is quite vocal. She expresses herself*

with a loud whinney. One day recently I drove a different car to the farm where I board them. Sunni was standing in a field adjacent to the driveway. I stood up by the driver's side of the vehicle and called her name. She threw up her head, looked all over, but couldn't see me. I then waved my hands, which immediately caught her attention, and she said her usual happy hello, loud and strong.

We never stop learning from each other, be it in or out of the saddle. I always try to return the love and trust they have shown me. When Marti had an accident and required fifteen stitches in her head, I was there to hold the light up and talk to her while the veterinarian repaired the damage. What a thrill it was for me to know that just my being there and talking to her helped to calm her down and relax while he completed the closing of the injury.

Through thick and thin, good times and bad, you can depend on a horse. All it requires is that you take the time to know them as individuals on a one-to-one basis.

Q. *I've heard there's a pet food company that puts out a free directory telling which hotels and motels accept pets. Is this true?* —P. N., INGLEWOOD, CALIF.

A. Yes and no. There is—but it isn't free. It costs fifty cents. It's called *Touring with Towser,* and you can get one by writing Gaines, TWT, P. O. Box 1007, Kankakee, Illinois 60901.

Q. *You never write about dog grooming. Why is it so expensive nowadays? And why do they do all those silly-looking cuts?* —G. C., YPSILANTI, MICH.

A. It's gone up, like everything else—among other reasons, because it's a tough job. If you don't believe it, try it yourself—on a poodle, say, or a Lhasa apso, or a Shih Tzu. And remember, dogs generally don't like it—at least not well enough to stand really still. I would compare it to a woman trying to work on a sewing machine, with the sewing machine on rollers.

As for the second of your questions, most groomers don't like those silly-looking cuts any more than you do. One trouble is that dog shows demand them. But one groomer I know, Jim Driver, actually refuses to do them. He believes, in no uncertain terms, that a dog should look the way God made it look.

Like all groomers, though, he's also had to live with some incredibly silly beliefs of his customers. One man told him he would never have a curly-haired dog; that all curly-haired dogs turned out to be mean. But the worst, Mr. Driver says, are the old wives' tales. One woman told him all dogs with black toenails have higher IQ's than dogs with light-colored toenails. Guess which color toenails her dog had?

Another woman said that a dog would never run away from home if you put a lock of its hair under the front porch. Mr. Driver, who grooms in the owners' own homes, took a look under the porch. Sure enough, there was the hair. When he looked for the dog, though—no dog. "He just runs away when he knows you're coming," the woman explained.

One day, while he was grooming another woman's dog, she became very angry when he told her her dog had fleas. "My dog is a purebred poodle," she said. "Purebred poodles don't get fleas."

"Maybe," suggested Mr. Driver, "they're purebred fleas."

Creature Comforts

Q. *Can any animal be housebroken?* —F. C., CROTON FALLS, N.Y.

A. No. If you don't believe it, try housebreaking a wolf, a coyote or a monkey. However, there are exceptions. I know one couple who even housebroke an elephant! It's a couple named Earl and Liz Hammond. They run an organization called Animal Kingdom Talent Services in Tioga, New York, and they are truly remarkable with animals. If you live in the West, you've seen Earl with a bear on those Hamm's beer commercials; he was also responsible for the original deer commercials for the Hartford Fire Insurance Company. Their elephant, whose name is Mignon, came from Thailand, and was so young when they got her she was actually raised in their house and even slept on a bed.

I was on "The Phil Donahue Show" once with her, and though it was an hour-long show and she had had a long wait before it, she didn't misbehave once until the director signaled we were off the air. Mignon is almost incredibly smart. Not long ago, when she was tied to her cable outside their house and Earl had gone inside, Mignon spotted the sledgehammer Earl had been using to build a fence. First Mignon went over to where the padlock of the cable was, picked it up with her trunk and held it on her front leg. Then she neatly picked up the sledgehammer, precisely smashed the padlock, and set herself free. After all that she didn't know where she wanted to go, so she just wandered around for about twenty minutes and then went inside to find Earl and Liz.

Q. *How do you train a cat?* —K. L., OAK FOREST, ILL.

A. It takes a lot of time and patience, but it's worth it, because after you're all finished you'll realize your cat has trained you to stop even trying. Cats don't "train." According to almost all cat authorities, although they are bright—the cats, I mean, not necessarily the authorities—cats do not know right from wrong, or at least human right from wrong. What they do know, and have a great desire for, is their own peace of mind. And they learn very quickly that they can have more of this by pleasing you than by vice versa. So they will honestly try to respect your wishes, idiotic as they may seem to them. Even the basics—litter box, scratching post, the difference between toys that are toys and things that would make excellent toys but, for some dumb reason of yours, are not—all can be taught by this method. You can say no to your cat and/or physically stop him from doing something. This is fine— but do it at the very moment. Afterward, it's meaningless to him. He cannot, or will not, then relate the punishment to the crime. In the immortal words of Doris Bryant, "There is no circumstance under which it is profitable to scold or punish a cat."

Q. *My dog's bark is worse than his bite. It's incessant. Even when*

friends come, he keeps barking until they sit down. What do I do? —P. H.,
WINDSOR, MO.

A. Put a chair for your guests right by the door. No, I'm kidding. The point is you *want* your dog to bark when someone comes to the door, but you also want him to *stop* after you've let the person in. This will take time and patience, and consistent and strict— but affectionate—discipline.

Outside of this kind of barking, which is the warning barking, your dog probably also barks when he's bored or lonely. Don't think, just because when you've had to leave him for the day you've left him on a trolley-run or even in the backyard, that alone will do the trick. It often won't. He can still get bored because he's alone. Try coming back in the middle of the day and surprising him in the middle of his bark. I don't mean the happy surprise barking when he sees you—that's fine. I mean the steady neighbor-annoying kind. Scold your dog when you've caught him in the act and, if necessary, put him inside for the rest of the day.

Whatever you do, do not use one of those "bark collars" you see advertised, which are supposed to give your dog a mild shock. They are fiendish. They do not give your dog a mild shock, they give him a terrible shock; and in some cases, they could make a cowering, psychological mess out of your dog for life. They can even be set off by another dog barking next door. They should be outlawed and you should write to any magazine that advertises them and tell the editors what you think of them for allowing such advertisements.

Q. *My cat only seems to want to play with things he shouldn't play with. What can I do?* —T. C., FULLERTON, CALIF.

A. Get him things to play with that he should play with. The easiest and best I've found is a large paper bag. He'll not only have a ball with it, so will you, just watching him. You may have to replace it from time to time, but he can think of things to do with a paper bag you won't believe.

Q. *My dog is constantly digging out of my yard. What can I do?*
—D. C., SEMINOLE, OKLA.

A. I presume he's digging underneath whatever fence you have. I suggest you get yourself a lot of chicken wire, at least one foot wide. Then take a hoe and scrape away until you can bury this fencing flat, but securely attached to the vertical fencing, and then cover it up with soil. My guess is your dog will soon believe he's fenced from underneath, too.

Q. *How do you keep a pet happy when you're out of your house or apartment?* —F. B., HULBERT, OKLA.

A. One way is by having at least two. The best idea, to my way of thinking, is to have a dog and a cat—preferably brought up together from puppyhood and kittenhood. Another way is to leave them something to play with. For a cat, a simple cloth ball is best. Still a third way is to leave on the radio, on an all-music station, turned low. Remember, your dog's hearing is at least seventeen times keener than yours, and your cat's is even keener. They don't need loud music—any more, for that matter, than they need you bellowing at them. I know one woman, Charlotte Schwartz of Cherry Hill, New Jersey, who runs a boarding kennel. She walks into a whole kennelful of barking dogs and literally just whispers, "Be quiet." It works, too—even though some kind of gradually quiet down with whisper barks. As for cats, one reason they come better to a woman's voice than to a man's is that it annoys them less.

Q. *My work-weary husband likes to watch TV in the evening, but we have an eight-month-old setter that will give him no peace. His incessant begging for attention is wearing our patience thin. What do we do?*
—O. R., COUNCIL BLUFFS, IOWA

A. Well, it shouldn't surprise you that after a long day of nothing to do your puppy isn't exactly eager to settle into an evening of sit-coms. Presumably he has no children or fellow dogs to romp with, and his day probably *begins* when you drop in at the end of yours.

At eight months, he's as full of energy and curiosity as a boy of five would be. To be blunt, his begging means he's bored. I'm willing to bet you a cat (and a cat might be a better pet in your situation) that after only fifteen or twenty minutes of really vigorous play—tug-of-war with an old towel, ball-chasing or wrestling—your dog would be perfectly content with dinner, a quiet evening and an occasional word or pat. (Who knows, maybe this little exercise regimen will have the same effect on your husband?)

Aside from the nuisance factor, your puppy must have at least that much activity each day or his body won't develop normally. In other words, it's not just something your dog needs psychologically, but actually physically.

Q. *My small son plays much too roughly with our new puppy. What can I do?* —K. T., KANSAS CITY, MO.

A. The best advice I can give you is to follow the example of the father of the man who became one of the most famous dog-story writers of all time: Albert Payson Terhune.

When Terhune was a small boy, his father discovered him "playing" with their new puppy. Young Terhune had picked up the puppy by the ears and was swinging him around.

Promptly, the father reached down and picked up Terhune by the ears and swung him around. Terhune always remembered how he had been not only surprised but also hurt. His father told him that the puppy had been, too.

Q. *My puppy won't eat dog food. He wants my food.* —R. L., ALEXANDRIA, VA.

A. Don't give it to him. You're giving him "people food" because you like to. You're rationalizing this by saying you are giving him variety. If you want to give him variety, mix his kibble and meat at all meals—just kibble in the morning and meat later may put him off his kibble. But don't—repeat, don't—give him snacks. If he's really off his—repeat, *his*—food, take him to the vet. Poor appetite is an early sign of a sick puppy.

Q. *How do you feel about people who come to your house and, after you've asked them not to, surreptitiously feed tidbits to your dog?* —C. M., MATAWAN, N.J.

A. I think it's a very wrong thing to do; and when I've been guilty of it—as we all have—I feel ashamed. When I'm on the other side and have asked people not to feed my dogs, and then have seen them do it, I'm angry. The whole thing boils down to the fact that if you don't have any real regard for the animal in question, at least you might have some respect for his or her owner. The momentary satisfaction you get and the idea that you're liked by the animal are both phony feelings. You are not only hurting the animal physically by giving him something that isn't good for him, you are doing something far worse: you are ruining his training and making him a nuisance, and starting something that, sooner or later, he will be punished for. And you're the one who should have been punished.

Q. *How can I keep ants, silverfish and other insects out of the house without putting out poison? I can't risk having my cats get into it.* —V.G., WACO, TEX.

A. If you're careful not to leave any open or sticky containers around, that will help—but there are also a couple of organic repellants you can try. For ants, mix coffee grounds with water and pour it down ant holes, and around the bases of the walls outside. For silverfish, try sprinkling Borax around the areas they frequent.

Q. *I've heard peanut butter kills birds because they cannot swallow it, and it gets stuck in their throats and they can't breathe. Is this true?* —F. N., MECHANICSBURG, PA.

A. No, many authorities recommend peanut butter in bird feeders.

Q. *Dogs seem to understand our words and commands better than cats. Do they really?* —M. F., JENKINS, KY.

A. I've told you before and I'll tell you again: your cat knows perfectly well what you want him to do—he just doesn't want to do it. Not only can cats understand words and commands better than dogs, they also have a sensitivity to your moods which is positively eerie. One man went so far as to say that his cat understood words so well he could differentiate btween *hungry*, *hurry*, and *Harry*. Well, maybe. But I'll bet his name was Harry, and that he rarely used the word *hurry*. And, knowing cats, if he did use the word *hurry*, it didn't do any good.

Q. *I have always owned dogs. Now I have a kitten. What general advice can you give me about (a) housebreaking, and (b) safety?* —N. C., NORTHERNAIRE, WIS.

A. Well, here are eight suggestions from Ralston Purina and the Cat Protection people. First, housebreaking:

Cats are by nature extremely—even fussily—clean animals. Housebreaking is seldom a problem. If you are training a new kitten, help him by placing him in his sanitary tray after meals, after periods of energetic play, first thing in the morning and last thing at night. Don't allow a new cat freedom of the house until you are sure he is using his tray regularly.

Enameled baking pans are easily kept clean and do not rust. Wash out with soap and hot water only. *Never use strong disinfectants.* Cat litter is excellent material to put in the tray and helps keep cat smell to a minimum. Newspaper is cheap, absorbant and easily disposable, but must be changed much more frequently than cat litter.

Second, safety precautions:

1. Flatten all tin cans and dispose of empty jars.
2. Keep all paint and varnish cans firmly shut.
3. Read labels of rodent or roach poisons before using. Many are highly toxic to domestic pets.
4. Consult your veterinarian before dosing your pet with any patent medicine.
5. Screen all windows. Cats are surefooted, but they may misjudge a jump. Don't take a chance.
6. Ribbons on the neck are dangerous, since they are easily caught and pulled tight. If your pet wears a collar outdoors for identification purposes, be sure it is large enough to slip over its head if necessary. A stretch-type collar is now available.
7. Be careful of open drawers, trunks and closets. Cats like warm, dark spots and are often unwittingly imprisoned.

And finally, from me, *don't de-claw*. If your cat gets out, he is helpless. If your furniture takes a beating, so be it. Your furniture is not alive; your cat is. Remember the man who was asked if his house was on fire and he could save only one of two possessions—a portrait by Rembrandt or his cat—which he would choose. Without hesitation, he chose his cat. And you're talking about a *sofa!*

Q. *My daughter keeps her two cats in an apartment all the time. They never get out. I think it's cruel. Do you?* —S. B., NEW YORK, N.Y.

A. No, I don't. I think as long as they have company—people who love them and other animals to play with—they are far better off than being permitted to get out, get terrified, get lost, and so on. Where can they go outside, anyway? In the street? In the back alleys? No, a city cat belongs in an apartment.

Q. *What do you think of (a) collars for cats, and (b) walking a cat on a leash?* —C. P., MT. PLEASANT, TENN.

A. There are very few cats who like collars—they are confining and they can also be dangerous. I don't like fancy collars for either dogs or cats. Anything that's really for you—or really, for your ego—rather than for your pet, I find offensive, and that goes for raincoats, booties and even those incredible little umbrellas. On the other hand, a small, simple collar can save your cat's life, if he or she gets lost, and if the collar includes your telephone number. I think the idea of walking a cat on a leash is okay, but only if your particular cat takes to it. And the chances are a hundred to one he won't. Also, walking him, you run the risk of ticks, worms, and similar problems. Cats, in my opinion, belong in the home and only in the home—and in a carefully screened home at that, so they can't get out. There is simply too much chance of too much misery outside.

Q. *Some time ago you wrote about walking cats on a leash. I just can't get my cat to do it.* —B. C., ALTADENA, CALIF.

A. You aren't the only one who wrote me such a letter. In fact, I got so many letters that one day when I saw a man walking a cat on a leash I stopped, got out of the car and accosted him. I told him about my column and asked him please to save me—how did he do it?

He told me his name was Alfredo Russo and he was a beauty shop operator. His cat was four years old. He started walking his cat on a leash just four months ago. He did so, he said, because he had moved from an area where the cat had been able to go out on his own to an area where that was simply impossible. There were just too many cars too close by.

Everything about the leash-walking, Mr. Russo told me, was difficult at the beginning—even getting the right harness. He practically had to make it himself. However, he believed, as I do, that a harness for a cat is vastly preferable to a collar.

Mr. Russo admitted that at the beginning his walks were almost total failures. Most of the time the cat wouldn't even budge from the doorstep. Then, suddenly, one day, Mr. Russo got an idea: not to pull, push or even try to coax the cat anywhere, but just to stand and wait and hold the leash loosely. Sure enough, when the cat realized he could decide where to go, the walks began to work.

There were still problems, Mr. Russo told me. A noisy car, two cars together, a motorcycle and many other things frighten the cat into immobility. When that happens, he picks it up and takes it in again. "He's a little scared now," Mr. Russo pointed out. "I don't know what it was this time. But each day he gets less scared."

Mr. Russo admitted he even had to cope with neighbors who told him that he was being either cruel or stupid, that you couldn't walk cats on leashes. One of his neighbors who told him that, however, doesn't tell him so anymore. The other day his cat, which had been allowed to go out by itself in the same area as Mr. Russo's, was run over and killed.

Q. *I am a single woman and I work. I want a cat and I can have it at my work. But my friends tell me that because I have to travel a lot, I shouldn't have a cat–that cats don't like to travel. What do you think?* —G. R., COVINGTON, VA.

A. It is true that cats don't travel well. But then neither do children and servants. Seriously, some cats are made miserable merely by having to change apartments, let alone lead a carrying-case life. But other cats, like most dogs, are better traveling with you than being left alone for a long time.

Your best bet is to get a kitten and start immediately to take it everywhere with you. Planes will be a problem. You can take your kitten in a carrying case, as long as the case will fit under the seat. But you can do this only if you advise the airline when you make your reservation, and they will permit only one animal per compartment (first class and tourist) per plane.

Your worst problem will be hotel rooms. When you go out of your room without your cat, leave it in the bathroom with a sign on the door. Otherwise it will shoot out the door the moment the maid opens it. I put the Do Not Disturb sign on the bathroom door when I occasionally find a stray cat in a strange city, and carefully add the words Dog inside. Why *dog?* Well, I figure that maids might be curious about a cat. Why don't I put the Do Not Disturb sign on the outside door? Well, I guess I just don't have *that* much faith in signs.

Q. *Is it true that one year of a dog's life equals seven years of our lives?* —F. R., HAMPTON, VA.

A. Not really. They now figure it this way: a six-month-old dog equals a ten-year-old child; a one-year-old dog, a fifteen-year-old; a two-year-old, a twenty-five-year-old. Today, according to tables prepared by Dr. Louis Vine, after your dog's first two years—the equivalent of twenty-five of yours, remember—each year for him is like four years for you.

Q. *Why do dogs and cats have so much better senses of smell than humans?* —M. B., WORCESTER, MASS.

A. Start with your nose versus your dog's nose. Although yours may be a pretty good size, it's not compared to all of you. And besides, four-fifths of it is taken up by parts that don't have any value when it comes to smelling. The part that contains your ethmoidal cells, essential for smelling, is about one and a half cubic inches. Your dog's is about six cubic inches. Put in numbers, you have 5 million ethmoidal cells and a dachsund has 125 million, a fox terrier 150 million and a German shepherd 200 million.

Just how remarkable your dog's sense of smell really is was proved in a test abroad. The dog was a setter. He was kept in a shed while the man who owned him started out into the woods with twelve other men, each man stepping exactly in the footprints of the man in front of him. The men walked many hundreds of yards. Then the man who owned the setter turned right, and five of the men followed, all continuing to step in the preceding man's footsteps. The six other men, including a man the dog knew almost as well as his own master, turned left. Then the setter was turned loose. It followed its master's steps perfectly and when it came to the parting of the ways, without a moment's hesitation turned right. Even identical twins have proved no threat either to a dog's or cat's uncanny sense of smell.

Q. *I know* why *my cat purrs, but* how *does he?* —L. L., LOCK-HART, TEX.

A. The idea, very simply, is that when your cat breathes air into his lungs it goes through what you might call his voice box—his vocal cords. But since he controls these vocal cords, he can still keep the air coming in but turn off the purr, as he does, for example, when he's had enough patting.

Q. *Why is it that a horse's ears will go back flat against his head when he's angry, but when my dog's ears go back, it's when I'm talking to him or patting him and he's pleased?* —R. D., OLD SAYBROOK, CONN.

A. My guess is you have a German shepherd, a terrier, a husky—a breed with some wolf in it. A horse puts his ears back as a protective reflex before he attacks—for example, by biting. So do some other nonwolf-breed dogs, as well as cats and, for that matter, primates. The wolf breed, however, signifies by its flat ears either submissiveness or happiness.

Ears are both very important and very sensitive instruments of detection for all animals, and a great deal can be learned about an animal's mood from them. When you're riding a horse, for example, and he shoots his ears forward, look out: there's a hazard ahead. On the other hand, when the horse puts one ear forward and keeps the other one back, that means something interesting, but not hazardous, is ahead.

As for deer, they actually scan—like radar—with each ear moving seemingly completely independently. So, for that matter, do cats. Most animals can detect different sounds at great distances.

Try something: put your hands in back of your ears, cupping your hands with your fingers close together. Now talk. See how clearly you hear? Now put your hands down. Talk again in the same tone. Not so clear, right? And now you know how to scan. Just like a cat.

Q. *How can I tell if a dog is going to be unfriendly?* —B. B., DEN-MARK, S.C.

A. Obviously, two ways: bared teeth or angry barking. Generally speaking, you should proceed with caution if a dog either stands still with a stiff "half-mast tail" or comes at you with his head lowered, his body in a crouch and his nose held close to the ground.

Q. *I know dogs know their names, but do cats?* —E. P., KEYPORT, N.J.

A. Yes, but. And the *but* is that many people name their pets, dogs as well as cats, names that are too hard—or, rather, not hard enough. What you need is distinctive-sounding names. Cats in general are very sensitive to sound, and will surely understand whatever name you give them—even if they also want you to understand that, at a particular moment, they don't want to answer to it. One woman, Patricia Sanford, writes that she named her two kittens Topaz and Amber, in honor of the color of their eyes. They knew the names, too. But they resolutely refused to honor, under those names, the "come" call. She then tried Martini and Manhattan. Still no dice. Finally, in desperation and with some humor, she tried calling one of the kittens O'Shaughnessy. It worked.

The other kitten was harder. No matter what name she tried, nothing seemed to work. However, while the struggle was going on, the kitten was so funny that one day she happened to say, "You're silly." Immediately, the name stuck. "From my experiences," she writes, "I have come to the conclusion that a cat will consider the name you wish to give it, and he will accept it or reject it, depending on whether or not he likes the sound of it."

Q. *I recently saw a newspaper picture of a cat eating corn-on-the-cob.*
I know cats are finicky; why do papers print these faked animal shots?
—W. B., PORT WASHINGTON, WIS.

A. It wasn't faked. The first time I saw a cat go bananas over
corn-on-the-cob I couldn't believe my eyes, either.

There are other highly unlikely cat favorites, too. Indeed,
stranger even than corn-on-the-cob is the average cat's affinity for
canteloupe-on-the-rind. No, I'm not kidding. See for yourself next
time you're serving either corn or canteloupe.

But you're right; cats *are* finicky. They expect their corn with
melted butter and a dash of salt—but don't like that gourmet touch
of salt on canteloupe.

Q. *My mother says I can get diseases from kissing my dog. I'm going*

to keep on doing it anyway. But, just between you and me, can I? —C. K., GRETNA, LA.

A. I'm not going to be popular with your mother on this one, but your mother is wrong. Your dog can get far more diseases from *you* than you can from *him*. And, as a matter of fact, you can get many more from kissing your girl. But, come to think of it, I'd just as soon not go into that, either. And so I'm assuming that, in your case, that problem is in the future. Actually, there are very few canine germs that can be spread by kissing. While I'm on this subject, however, I get many questions about dogs getting "lifetime" shots for distemper, hepatitis, leptospirosis, and so on. There is no such thing as a lifetime shot for your dog. Whether or not he or she has contact with other dogs, your dog must have an annual booster shot.

Q. *I know that having a wet, cold nose is a sign of good health in my dog. Is the same thing true for my cat?* —L. Q., BATAVIA, OHIO

A. No, it is not true for your cat, and as a matter of fact, it isn't even a sign of good health for your dog—or at least not necessarily so. Not only can climatic conditions outside the house and atmospheric and humidity conditions inside the house affect the nose temperature of a perfectly healthy animal, there are also certain minor ailments of the respiratory tract that can give your dog a very cold nose, when, in fact, what he has is a cold.

Q. *I have heard of a dog with distemper being "quarantined" with cats. I was told dogs didn't get cats' diseases and cats didn't get dogs'. Is that really true?* —B. O'B., MANSON, WASH.

A. It is generally true, but *generally* is a big word. Distemper can't be passed from dog to cat, or vice versa, but certain rare diseases can—tuberculosis for one, rabies for another, and certain types of sarcoptic mange for a third. Also, and perhaps principally, ringworm can. Then there are the twilight areas. Dog fleas, for example, will attack cats, but prefer dogs. They will also attack people, but again they prefer dogs. Cat fleas, on the other hand, will attack dogs and sometimes people, but prefer cats. Who can blame them?

Q. *My cat is forever shaking his head and wiggling his ears. His hearing is all right, and he is otherwise normal. So what is he doing?* —T. C., COLUMBUS, NEB.

A. Unless he's trying to break into show business, I'd guess what he has is ear mites. These are small but dangerous parasites common in cats. You can't see them—except for an odd coloration on the inside of the ear—but the cat can certainly feel them, and they're probably driving him crackers. Get him to the vet; if left untreated, they'll make your cat deaf.

Q. *My cat has a dry, brittle coat and always has had. He gets plenty of fat from his canned meat, and I brush him regularly. What does he need?* —D. M., CAMDEN, N.J.

A. Maybe he needs a visit to the vet. With dogs and cats, any internal disorder they may have—even an inherited one—will show up first in the coat. To begin with, it will lose its shine.

If, on the other hand, your cat is one of the rare specimens whose coat was never meant to be glossy, you might experiment for a week by giving him a bit of egg—cooked, never raw—every couple of days. You're almost sure to notice a difference, provided he is otherwise in perfect health.

Q. *Are cats particularly prone to kidney disease?* —T. C., MODESTO, CALIF.

A. Well, male cats are more likely to suffer from this complaint than females. What can happen is that a speck of sand or dirt lodged in your cat's urethra can cause internal blockage and, ultimately, severe kidney damage. You don't have much time on the *ultimately*, either. If your cat seems to be having trouble urinating, to be spending excess time on his litter pan, to be licking more than usual, or to exhibit any other signs of distress, get him to your vet immediately. A mere seventy-two hours in obtaining treatment can make the difference between a fairly routine and simple procedure and a potentially tragic situation in which no treatment will work.

Q. *What is the truth about rabies in dogs?* —C. R., NEW ORLEANS, LA.

A. The truth is it's the most exaggerated disease there is. A dog may have a convulsion, a spasm, anything which makes it froth at the mouth—from epilepsy to indigestion—and people will scream, "Mad dog," "Shoot it," and then rush to the nearest hospital for vaccinations against rabies.

In point of fact, the number of cases of rabies in man, as reported by the Public Health Service in its Morbidity and Mortality Annual Supplement for the year 1970, was exactly two. Two cases! Out of a population of over two hundred million people!

I am indebted to a reader for bringing to my attention a quotation about rabies from Charles W. Dulles, a well-known Philadelphia physician and surgeon and lecturer at the University of Pennsylvania on the history of medicine. "I might cite," he said, "my own experience in the treatment of persons bitten by dogs supposed to be rabid, which has furnished not a single case of the developed disease in thirty years, and I have probably seen more cases of so-called hydrophobia than any other medical man."

Q. *Do cats need milk?* —P. R., EDGARTOWN, MASS.

A. Kittens, yes. But the prevailing opinion among vet-erinarians today is that milk is not essential to an adult cat's health and in no case should be substituted for water. All animals need water—even camels.

Q. *Do vegetarians ever insist that their pets be vegetarians, too?* —B. H., RICHMOND, IND.

A. More do than you might think. Gary Null, for example, does. He is the nutritionist who at twenty-six has been called "the major spokesman of the health food industry." He told me he has four Afghans, all of whom are fed only a special health food prepa-ration of his own—one that includes no meat, which he doesn't eat, either, but that does include garlic pearls, which, he says, kill worms. His dogs are in excellent health and apparently do not miss a meat diet at all, even though, since none of them came from special kennels or pet shops, but from shelters, they once ate meat. Mr. Null, incidentally, has had many kinds of dogs, but is now the compleat Afghan man. "Most people," he told me, "treat their dogs like children. Even with young Afghans, you can't do that. You have to treat them like adults. And you cannot make them love you, either. You cannot even mold their personalities, the way you can collies or boxers. You must simply accept them and love them for what they are."

By the way, here is a recipe for vegetarian dog biscuits, courtesy of the Fund for Animals and Beauty Without Cruelty:

3½ cups whole meal flour, including 2 whole wheat, 1 rye, ½ corn meal
2 cups cracked wheat, for texture
½ cup sesame seed for calcium
4 tsp. dulse, kelp or salt
½ cup brewers' yeast
1 pint vegetable stock or water
1 egg

Dissolve yeast in ¼ cup water, mix with stock, combine with other ingredients. Knead three minutes, roll to ¼-inch thickness, cut with cookie cutter, place on oiled baking sheet and bake in 300° F oven for 45 minutes. Turn off heat and leave in oven overnight.

I'm no cook, but it does sound delicious, doesn't it—particularly when you get to the part about that cookie cutter?

Q. *Somebody told me horses need more food in cold weather. Do they?*
—S. J., PONTIAC, MICH.

A. Yes—about fifteen pounds of good hay per day, plus an extra amount of grain. And there is a sad side to it. This winter, with the high price of beef, lamb, pork, and so on, as well as the high price of hay, the "killer" buyers, as the people who buy for horsemeat are called, have not only bought the lame, the halt and the old, they've also bought young horses for their "tender" meat. It's valuable both for the pet food industry and for people food, too—particularly in France. Even riding stables have been heavy sellers; they didn't want to have to feed their horses all winter. However, sad side aside, this was shortsighted of them. Since it takes an average of five years to school a saddle horse for beginning riders, come spring there are going to be a lot of beginners taking spills from—well, kindergarten horses.

Q. *Is it all right to give my guinea pig a bath? My mother always says I need one more than he does.* —M. P., SALEM, OHIO

A. Bathing your guinea pig is okay and, unlike you, he'll love it—especially a warm bath (but not too warm). Use a mild, white soap, rinse him twice in clear water and bathe him no more than twice a week. Between baths you should keep him clean by brushing him (gently).

And don't forget to tell your mother I told you to wash out the tub afterward!

Q. *My dog really suffers from the heat. What should I do?* —R. J., PROVIDENCE, R.I.

A. A lot of dogs do. And not just the big dogs like Saint Bernards, huskies, and so forth. Little dogs can have just as hard a time. Remember, they're so close to the pavement, and that hot

pavement can actually burn their paws. Speaking of paws, after you've come in from a walk, first give your dog some water—not too much—and let him put his paws in the water. Later you can make an ice pack with a towel and use that to cool those paws.

Dogs don't sweat, you know. They cool themselves by panting. And if they're really hyperventilating—overpanting—look out; particularly with the pushed-in-face dogs like boxers, Pekes and pugs. These can easily get heat stroke. If you believe your dog is really overpanting, take him to the vet. If you can't do that, take his temperature. If it's over 106, get him in a cold tub immediately.

Q. *My dog has bad breath. What do I do?* —F. A., CORFU, N.Y.

A. You're his best friend—tell him. No, I'm kidding. First, try brushing his teeth. Biscuits and bones won't do the job. Your dog won't like it much, but if you start early and make a game out of it—or at least, some fun—you can do it. Never mind the fancy toothpaste, either. Use plain salt solution, and a very soft brush or a piece of cotton. What this will do is to keep down the plaque— the film on the teeth—which later leads to more tartar and, just like with humans, to periodontitis.

I know of a man whose German shepherd was brought up from puppyhood to have his teeth brushed regularly. Every night, after his dinner, the shepherd would come to him and sit on a box so his master would not even have to lean down. The dog would open his mouth, pull back his lips and look for all the world like he was actually smiling. The toothpaste, incidentally, got all over everything but it was no problem—the dog cleaned it up.

If you try brushing but you can still hang your hat on your dog's breath, take him to the dentist. And this time I'm not kidding.

There are vets who specialize in dentistry. Dr. Worth Lanier, for example, advises that if a puppy's puppy teeth do not fall out on schedule and by the time the puppy is nine months old, they should be extracted.

Third, and finally, if neither brushing nor dentistry helps, take your dog to your regular vet. Bad breath could mean anything from roundworms to kidney disorder.

Q. *What is the cheapest form of animal birth control?* —P. J., AVON, CONN.

A. Buy a leash and never let your animal off it when he or she is outside, except in a run where your pet is alone or where you can watch it every minute. But the key word here is *never*.

Q. *Aside from spaying and neutering, is there any hope for a cheaper animal birth control method soon? Pills? In food? Injection? What?* —M.S., LISBON, OHIO

A. There is, and there isn't. Pills have been promised, but they also promise difficulty—if, in no other way, in the problem of remembering, daily, to give them. Putting the medicine in dog and cat food also is a problem—a lot of people eat those foods, too. The sterilization of males isn't the answer, either; just one unsterilized rover can impregnate so many females.

The most promising area of research lies in the control of the estrous cycle ("coming into heat") of the female. Dr. Kenneth Laurence of the Population Council at New York's Rockefeller University and Dr. Lloyd Faulkner at Colorado State Veterinary School are using immunological approaches.

Another development comes from San Francisco, where the Agrophysics Company has developed a breeding control device which many veterinarians in the area are now successfully installing in female dogs. Neither surgery nor drugs is necessary; it is painless and can be installed in just a few moments. At the University of Virginia, Dr. Charles Hamner has come up with an implant method which, inserted into the female dog's flank, prevents the dog from coming into heat for as long as five years. The animal need not be anesthetized, but merely tranquilized, to do the job.

Q. *What can I say to people who say I am odd for having had my tomcat neutered?* —M. C., HASTINGS, N.Y.

A. You can tell them that you're not the odd one; they are. You are just trying to even the odds against your cat adding to the awful overpopulation problem.

You might even try humor. You could do worse than use the story Hames Humes writes about in his book *Podium Humor*.

Humes writes of a public relations consultant who was once asked to define just what a consultant was. The man said the best definition had been given by a neighbor of his in Scarsdale, New York, whose family pet was a very vocal tomcat. Every evening the block was accustomed to hearing this cat give oral evidence that he was indeed the cat's meow.

One day, on the morning train to New York, the consultant saw his neighbor and told him he had noticed that the cat had been quiet lately.

"Well," said the friend, "I took the hints of friends like you and had him neutered."

"Oh," the first man said. "I bet he spends his nights now sitting on the hearth in front of the fire."

"No," replied the owner, "he still goes out. But, like you, he now goes along as a consultant."

Q. *Can spayed or neutered pets still enjoy sex?* —F. R., LAKE PLACID, NEW YORK

A. You've actually got a couple of questions going there. In the first place, your dog or cat just isn't into, as the expression goes, sex for sex's sake. It mates in response to hormonal clues designed by nature strictly for reproduction. If your pet undergoes an ovariohysterectomy (spaying) or castration (neutering), the hormones go—and any desire to mate goes with them. I have heard of occasional cases in which a male cat or dog, neutered later than usual in life, has continued to exhibit some spraying or mating behavior out of habit. But not for long.

There are surgical procedures that, unlike spaying or neutering, prevent conception but leave the parasexual traits intact. A vasectomized male, for example, will continue to pine away down the block—and if he's a cat, he'll still spray your furniture—while a female with tubal ligation will still go into heat and cause a furor in the neighborhood.

All of these operations obviously do the job of combating one of today's greatest cruelties—unwanted animals. But the great advantage of spaying and neutering is that they alone remove these parasexual traits and also the possibilities of some disease. Your male pet fights less and stays home—out of danger—more. And your female has far less chance of developing cancer of the breast and will not, of course, develop cancer of the uterus or uterine infections. She also will not die giving birth to pups or kittens. Which, sadly, isn't as uncommon as you might think.

Q. *What should you do when you see a dog or a cat on the highway?*
—P. M., SAN DIEGO, CALIF.

A. If it's injured, pick it up as best you can. Put it in your car and take it to the nearest veterinarian. If he's the kind, as some are, who won't look at it until he sees cash, tell him it's your animal.

If the dog or cat is not injured, the chances are you'll probably have to keep going, turn off the road and double back on it. Approach slowly, stop your car (off the road!) and try to entice the animal into your car. A dog will often get into your car when he wouldn't come to you in person. If that doesn't work—or if the animal is a cat—get out of your car and approach the animal in such a way that if he turns and runs he doesn't run out into traffic.

If the animal is in the middle of the road, or, worst of all, on an island between lanes, you've probably got to get help to stop the traffic. Some policemen are understanding about animal rescuers, some are not. Many do not know that there is such a thing as a Good Samaritan law. Barry Farber, the radio commentator, was responsible for it in New York. It helps you if you're trying to do a good deed.

Q. *What's the best way to subdue an injured animal if it absolutely must be moved? When they're in great pain, they're almost impossible to approach.* —I. H., WEST POINT, N.Y.

A. Well, first and foremost, the animal should be moved and shifted around as little as possible, particularly if he is bleeding internally (check the inner eyelid for paleness) or has broken bones. That means he should be slid onto a stiff surface, like a canvas stretcher or a plywood board, before he is transported.

The best way of quietening the animal is by covering him with a heavy blanket, like an army blanket. Place it gently over the animal and then tuck it around him, covering as much of the head as he will allow. The blanket should soothe him, and will also prevent him from thrashing around, reduce the effects of shock, and keep you from being bitten.

Q. *Is it sensible to give mouth-to-mouth resuscitation to an animal that has stopped breathing? I know their respiratory systems are different from ours.* —H. J., ALEXANDRIA, VA.

A. It's definitely sensible, and usually works like a charm. You must blow into the animal's nose, however, and not into his mouth, and the process is most successful when accompanied by manipulation of the chest cavity. When you blow in, grab and lift the skin around the rib cage. Press to expel the air. And if you are reluctant to put your mouth on the animal's nose, use your cupped hand as a funnel.

In any case, try. You can save an animal's life with little or no risk to yourself.

Q. *We're into the hot weather now. What can I do if I find a dog or cat locked in a car and really suffocating?* —F. E., CRAIG, COLO.

A. Your power to *re*act is boundless. Your power to *act*, however, is limited. Of five states surveyed—California, Florida, Massachusetts, Michigan and New York—only one provides that a person can feed or water the animal. But this same law, Section 356 of New York's Agriculture and Markets law, also says that over twelve hours must have passed before such action can be taken.

In Massachusetts, you should be especially cautious as a would-be Good Samaritan. Chapter 49, Section 40 of the Massachusetts statutes states that anyone who "rescues beasts lawfully restrained or impounded shall be liable to any person injured for all damages sustained."

Massachusetts, Michigan and Florida present little relief for either the person noticing the distressed animal or the animal. The owner of the animal, when found, can be prosecuted for cruelty. But a bystander who decides to play Boy Scout could find himself facing criminal charges because he is liable for trespassing or liable for damages resulting from the break-in.

If the animal is *in extremis*, is might be possible for a police officer to seize the animal. According to Bill Blumenschein of the New York district attorney's office, such a seizure would be legal.

But beware of the consequences. If the animal is unclaimed, it could be euthanized.

If the car is unlocked, is there an owner alive who would object to giving the animal a bit of water? As for rolling down the windows, perhaps it is best that you make sure the animal cannot jump out, and that you stay there to keep potential car thieves from jumping in!

Animals Have Rights, Too!

Q. *Is it true that bullfighting got you involved in animal work?*
—DR. G. L., PITTSBURGH, PA.

A. Yes. The very first one I ever saw in Nogales, Mexico, literally changed my life. Not just because of the horrible fights that memorable bloody Sunday, but also through my trip the next day to an Arizona public library. Here I found eighteen books on the bullfight, every single one of them entirely favorable.

Apologists would have you believe that the bullfight is steeped in antiquity and hallowed by tradition. The fact is that it is steeped all right, and even hallowed—but not quite in the kind of antiquity and tradition its promoters have in mind. Not in that library but elsewhere, I found a book by Captain Basil Hall entitled *Extracts from a Journal Written on the Coasts of Chile, Peru and Mexico.* In this extract, a Chilean told Captain Hall:

> *The Spaniards had systematically sought by these cruel shows, and other similar means, to degrade the taste of their Colonies, and thereby more easily tyrannize over the inhabitants. The people, first rendered utterly insensible to the feelings of others by a consistant familiarity with cruelty and injustise to animals, soon became indifferent to the*

wrongs of their country and lost, in the end, all motive to generous exertion in themselves.

Sooner or later, you will inevitably be referred to what all *aficionados* regard as their Bible: Ernest Hemingway's *Death in the Afternoon.* "So far, about morals," Hemingway writes, "I know only that what is moral is what you feel good after and what is immoral is what you feel bad after." The kindest comment would seem to be that perhaps Mr. Hemingway has his morality confused with his digestion. In any case, if he is remarkable about morality, he is even more remarkable on the subject of the horses—the death of the bull in the ring, Mr. Hemingway maintained, is tragic, the death of the horse *comic!*

Years ago Spain's most famous horse contractor for the bullfights was a man named Antonio Cruz. Señor Cruz was famed for his ability to patch up even the most badly wounded horse, so that it could make at least one more appearance in the bullring. In one description he "stuffed their guts back into their bellies with a fist," then sewed them up with a needle and twine. If, in this work, there were any unsightly loose ends, the señor would cut them off with a pair of scissors. All in all, he was very proud of his handiwork. "No vet ever touched my horses," he later boasted. "I did it all myself. I really understood horses."

Under the government of Primo de Rivera, the Spaniards finally decided to attempt to protect the horses with a kind of quilted mattress cover. However, it should be noted that this was done only, in the exact words of the decree, to avoid "sights which so disgust foreigners and tourists." In other words, such sights did not, apparently, disgust Spaniards. Unfortunately, the bull has little difficulty getting his horns underneath the covering. Today it is rare that you will see a *corrida* without at least one brutal goring. The horses are supposed, incidentally, to have one eye blindfolded so that they cannot see as the bull charges them, but can see to be ridden around the ring. In practice this regulation is a dead letter; both eyes are usually covered. Often horses are doped or their vocal cords are cut, or both.

If bullfighting is indefensible in regard to horses, what of the bull himself? The *aficionado* will talk to you for hours of the way bulls are bred; of how they are tested for bravery by being lanced on the ranch as calves; of how, when they reach fighting age, they can split a leaf with their horns, charge a train, beat a lion or a tiger, and so on and on. If you have the misfortune to go to a bull-fight, however, I guarantee that for every bull you see who exhibits even a nodding acquaintance with such fearsome qualities, you will see at least three whose only desire is to get out of the ring.

The plain and simple fact of the matter is that the brave bull the *aficionados* so pride themselves on is not only well down the line in animal IQ, he ranks, as a fighting animal, as very possibly the stupidest there is. After all, does it make sense that a brave bull would time and time again charge a silly, waving cloth instead of going after the source of all his misery and torment—the man. It is interesting to note that the kind of *aficionado* who adores telling you how the brave bull can beat a lion or a tiger has never, to anyone's knowledge, shown even the slightest inclination to get into a ring with any other kind of an animal—be it anything from a guard dog to a cross goose.

Q. *Why is Alaska such a cruel state?* —W. G., SEAFORD, DEL.

A. Cruelty to animals runs throughout Alaska's history. The first white men to arrive there were the Russians, who specialized in slaughtering sea otters, seals and Aleuts. Eventually, they combined the latter two and put what Aleuts they hadn't slaughtered on the Pribilof Islands, where they used them as slaves, and where, to this day, they continue to slaughter seals for us.

After the Russians came the Americans—or, rather, American whalers. These whalers, ironically, weren't after whales but baleen; but the trouble was that the baleen, a flexible, horny substance, was located in the mouths of bowhead whales.

The whales used it to strain food from sea water. The white men used it to make corset stays for women.

In 1850, it cost 32¢ a pound; in 1905, $4.80. The rest of the whale in those days wasn't worth much, and when a substitute for baleen was found—for women's corsets, don't forget—Alaskan whaling ended.

Q. *I have two questions about coyotes. I heard about a recent hunt in Colorado where hunters took dozens of dogs out on trucks and then set them on any coyotes they found. Aren't there laws to stop such things? My second question is, can a coyote be made a pet?* —S. K., HOT SPRINGS, ARK.

A. In answer to your first question, there are laws, but they are not enforced. However, the Fund for Animals has made a standing offer of one hundred dollars to anyone who supplies prior information on, and contributes material support to, the prevention or stopping of any such hunt by any means short of actual violence. In answer to your second question, there are many people who have made successful pets of coyotes. Others have preferred to leave the coyote where he is and simply make friends with him. One such man is Gerald Coward of Los Angeles, a photographer and writer. He once met a coyote on a walk up a canyon, and for two and a half years he took the same walk every day and each time met the same coyote. They played and romped together and then, at the end of the day, said good-bye. When the coyote mated, he brought his mate to meet Mr. Coward. It was a remarkable idyll that lasted until a massive fire raged around the Los Angeles area, after which Mr. Coward saw his coyote no more. "The coyote," he says with conviction, "is the greatest animal there is."

Q. *Is it true people still hunt polar bears?* —J. M., FT. MORGAN, COLO.

A. Yes—but only in Canada. Polar bears inhabit Alaska, Canada, Norway, Greenland (i.e., Denmark) and Russia, and all but Canada have agreed to stop hunting them. Russia, in fact, was the first to do so, in 1957. Now, to its shame, Canada is the only one left. The polar bears that are still hunted are in Canada's Northwest Territories. Here, Canada allows Eskimos and Indians to kill the bears. They can either kill them themselves or sell their right to kill a bear—for $2500. Since if they killed the bears themselves, the most they would get would be $200 per bear, you can imagine who gets almost all the rights to kill the big white. The big white hunter, of course.

A LETTER-OF-THE-WEEK *from Bangkok, Thailand:*

> *In regard to your opinion of* Jaws, *I have lived in Thailand for several years, and even here people are aware of the "American disease," as you make it out to be, of shark-killing. Unfortunately, this may rapidly become a world disease.*
>
> *But people in Thailand are far less naive than Americans; they have lived for centuries with dangerous animals around them. Take the matter of snakes. There are many, many poisonous snakes in Thailand. Thousands of people used to be bitten every year by them and a couple of hundred people died every year as a result. But the Thai answer was not to go out and kill every snake they could get their hands on. It was first to learn something about snakes—which ones are poisonous and which are not—and second to install, all over the country, a chain of Serum Centers. Wherever a person goes in the country now, he is not far from a Serum Center. And fatalities from snake bites are way down.*
>
> JAMES ROONEY

Q. *Is it true that Australia has banned the export of kangaroo products?* —E. S., GREENWOOD, MISS.

A. Yes, it has; hides and meat. And the action by the Labour Party government of Prime Minister Gough Whitlam was particularly encouraging news because Liberal governments have not always been as concerned with animal issues as have Conservative ones. Also, the action was closely followed by an announcement from our own Department of the Interior that it intended to declare the kangaroo an endangered species. For years the kangaroo, the national symbol of Australia—a gentle, almost defenseless animal—has been killed in a sadistic carnage of maimed mothers and bashed babies, or *joeys*. "Pouch joeys," Charles Baines wrote me, "are ground under the heel of a boot. Hopping joeys are swung by the tail and their heads bashed against the nearest tree." About three-quarters of this slaughter was to provide pet food, leather, fur coats and cuddly toys including, of all ironies, toy koala bears. The other quarter was divided between "control" and "sport." In this country, the pelts were processed by two firms, William Amer of Philadelphia and Ziegal Eisman of Rahway, New Jersey. The Fund for Animals led the fight for the kangaroo in this country, but prime credit for the ban should go to Australia's own Eve Fesl, Marjorie Wilson, Nan Ingleton and Mr. Baines, of the Save the Kangaroo Committee.

Q. *I read that there are only an estimated twenty or so panthers in Florida, but that there are over fifty thousand alligators. And yet both are classed as endangered and can't be harmed. I don't understand it and I'm suspicious. What good is an alligator?* —W. L., PRICHARD, ALA.

A. Numbers have very little to do with endangerment. Obviously, the handful of panthers is endangered. But so, too, is the seemingly plentiful alligator. One open-season's "bag"—or opportunity to make shoes and bags out of them—could easily wipe out all the alligators. What good do alligators do? For one thing, they actually supply water. In a state like Florida, where there are only two seasons, the short wet and the long dry, "gator holes," as they are called, may be the only permanent year-round answer. The alligator literally digs his own water holes—and broad, deep pools they are, too. For a second thing, alligators protect bird rookeries. They themselves don't get to the birds' eggs in large numbers, and yet their very presence around the rookeries keeps away other predators that would destroy the eggs. Finally, like so many animals—particularly ones as interesting as the alligator—they are a terrific tourist attraction. But just being wanted to be seen by tourists presents danger. Remember in the old days people used to say, Children should be seen and not heard? Well, for nowadays, how about trying this: animals should be seen and not hurt.

Q. *I've read the "defense" of the American Museum of Natural History's horrible cat experiments, and I simply can't believe it. Do people really justify such cruelty?* —V. B., WESTPORT, CONN.

A. When the Museum story first broke and it became obvious that the New York museum had received half a million dollars over sixteen years for a weird variety of freakish sex experiments—cats were blinded, deafened, made unable to smell, had parts of their penises cut off, etc., all so that their ability to perform sexually could be measured "scientifically"—there was an immediate outburst of fury on the part of all decent people all over the country. On one talk-back radio program, which went to thirty-six states, Helen Jones and I answered questions for two hours—and not a single caller defended the experiments.

But the defense came, make no mistake. These defenses run a pattern. First, a humane society that can be counted on not to rock any boats—in this case, New York's ASPCA—is invited to "tour" the experiment, but they do not get to see the actual experiment, of course, and then issue a statement giving the "facilities" a clean bill of health. Next, one of the big shots in the experiment, in this case the Director of the Museum, issues a statement that "research on animals benefits all of us," and that he has invited the ASPCA, the Department of Agriculture's Veterinary Inspection Service, and the National Institutes of Health's Animal Welfare Office to see the facility and that none of them has been "dissatisfied." The New York *Daily News* not only printed the Director's release verbatim but also editorialized that "animal lovers" were "hysterical," that "research benefits"—in capital letters—"MILLIONS OF LIVES," and that there were "humane standards set down by such organizations as the National Institutes of Health, the American Physiology Society and the American Psychological Association."

This is, of course, absurd. Those groups are the actual experimenters—it would be like getting Jesse James to set the standards for bank security. And to say that such research benefits all of us goes against the statements issued by the experimenters themselves: Dr. Lester Aronson, who is "Curator of the Museum's Department of Animal Behavior" and his "Research Fellow," Madeline Cooper, both of whom have admitted that they base their defense on their right—at a museum, mind you—to do anything, whether or not it has any benefit or application for anything.

All in all, it reminds me all too vividly of the defense put up by Wayne State University in Detroit when they were battering dogs' heads with pneumatic hammers. What for? For cancer? For heart trouble? For *any* disease? No, for football helmets!

Incidentally, neither Dr. Aronson nor any other official of the Museum was willing to debate me on ABC's "Good Morning, America." However, the National Society for Medical Research procured Dr. Clarence Dennis, of the Veterans' Administration Hospital in Northport, New York, to do so. Since Dr. Dennis declared he did not have "full data" on the Museum's experiments, I brought up one at Dr. Dennis's own hospital. This was an experiment called "A Note on an Attempt to Induce a Schizophreniclike State in Kittens." In this experiment, I noted that, according to the Official Report in the *Journal of Genetic Psychology*, 5,000 electrical shocks were given to the "experimental kittens" seven days after birth and continuing for the next thirty-five days. I quote the *Journal* further:

> *The behavior of the mother cat, although not part of the experiment, merits attention. . . . When she eventually discovered that the experimental kitten was being given electric shocks during the feeding process or whenever it was close to her body, she would do everything possible to thwart the experimenters with her claws, even trying to bite the electrodes off. She would run over to the kitten, trying to feed it or else comfort it as much as possible.*

Maybe that benefits "MILLIONS OF LIVES" too.

Q. *How did prairie dogs get their name? What is being done to save them?* —G. B., PITTSTON, PA.

A. Prairie dogs got their name because they live on the prairies and behave like dogs—which is to say, they are sociable, friendly, intensely curious little guys who wag their tails and bark when they are excited. They are also intelligent and well disciplined, banding together to guard their "dog towns," stand sentry duty, and so forth. In the 1930s, they were poisoned by the millions under the auspices of the federal government's despicable Wildlife Services. Finally, in February 1972, President Nixon's widely praised executive order banned the use of "secondary" poisons—the chain reaction ones (1080, thalium, strychnine)—on public lands. However, two years later, the Interior Department's Sport Fisheries and Wildlife Commission announced it planned to poison more than thirteen thousand acres of federal, state and private lands. But this action, in direct conflict with President Nixon's order, has so far been thwarted, largely due to the work of the Fund for Animals, Friends of the Earth and other groups.

In Amarillo, Texas, some years ago, prairie dogs which had escaped the poisoning took possession of a ten-acre vacant lot. A Presbyterian Children's Home was located on part of the lot. The home people decided not to destroy the prairie dogs, and it soon turned out to be a wise decision. Like the dogs, the orphaned and deprived children had also had their little worlds overturned, and they took not only renewed heart but also important therapeutic solace from their association with the brave little prairie dogs. Today, sadly, Amarillo's "dog town" is gone—an expressway came through—and the few remaining dogs had once more to move. And now the children's home, dogless, is that much more forlorn.

Q. *I can't stand reading about the killing of all the whales. How many are left? What is being done about it? What can one person do?*
—M. S., BARDSTOWN, KY.

A. The lastest authoritative figures for remaining great whales are as follows: for the gray (Atlantic), extinct; for the gray (Pacific), 8,000 to 10,000; for the right whale (Southern), 80 to 150; for the right whale (Arctic), 100 to 500; for the blue whale, 600 to 1500; for the humpback, 1500 to 2000. What is being done about it is that the United States government has called a ten-year moratorium on the killing of whales. Nonetheless, the slaughter continues, principally by Japan and Russia, but also by Norway, where the infamous International Whaling Commission has its headquarters.

One person can do a lot. He or she can not only join one of the international societies doing something about the whale, but he or she can also join the boycott already underway against Japan and Russia, organized by the Fund for Animals. For further information, we suggest you write to the Fund for Animals, 140 West 57th Street, New York, New York 10019.

Q. With all that's been written about the "whale marches," why doesn't someone tell the story of what happened to the "humane" harpoon? To me, it's the worst thing about the whole rotten business. —F. J., CORAL GABLES, FLA.

A. I agree. The "humane"—or electric—harpoon, far better in every way than the excruciatingly cruel explosive harpoon, was invented by an Englishman named Day. It was tried out during an Antarctic whale slaughter.

The gunner used was a crack Norwegian shot who was so proficient that, using the explosive harpoon, he was able to hit approximately ninety-seven per cent of his targets. Although the electric harpoon shot even more accurately, when the same Norwegian gunner used it he kept missing. Indeed, he only hit forty per cent of his targets.

Immediately after this, the electric harpoon was abandoned. The whole episode was so unbelievable that few people were surprised when it was later charged that the Norwegian gunner was actually working for the inventor of the explosive harpoon, who got a certain amount of money every time his invention was fired.

In such a way was the humane harpoon itself harpooned, and once again it was proved that money may or may not be the root of all evil, but it certainly is the root of most cruelty to animals.

There is another whale story you may not have heard. It is the story of one whaling captain who, like so many of his breed, thought nothing of harpooning a pregnant whale. But his crew had

trouble getting the whale aboard, and as two of them were manipu-
lating the two chains around the huge tail, the pressure caused the
fetus inside, weighing more than two tons, to be suddenly ex-
pelled. It literally shot out of the mother whale, and, striking the
captain right in the face, took his head clean off.

Please omit flowers.

Q. *I heard the Navy is still trying to make dolphins into kamikazes.
The Navy says it isn't. What's the story?* —J. W., JEFFERSONVILLE, IND.

A. While the Navy may be technically right in saying they are
not making dolphins into actual kamikazes, a technicality is just
what it is. The Navy is engaged in a huge program, using not only
dolphins as "weapons systems," but also pilot whales and killer
whales. If you don't believe it, ask Michael Greenwood, now a
college professor in Minnesota. He's the man who worked for ten
years as a senior researcher on dolphins for the Navy, and recently
blew the whistle on the whole rotten business.

Afterward he told a Fund for Animals' meeting in New York
that dolphins are being used in four ways. The first is in a "swimmer deterent system"—which is Navy euphemese for killing
enemy swimmers, and was actually used in Vietnam. In this the
dolphin is fitted with a nose-cup to which is attached a lance to
which, on the other end, is attached a syringe. When the dolphin
rams the target, the syringe releases a high-pressure gas that causes
collapse of the stomach and intestines. The second way is a "back
pack system," in which the dolphin wears a saddle over his dorsal
fins and carries anything from an instrumentation system to, theo-
retically, explosives. This is better than the nose-cone system, from
the Navy's point of view, because it doesn't inhibit the dolphin's
sonar capabilities. Its disadvantage, like the nose-cup lance, is that
it can be seen. The third use of the dolphin is to convert him into a
"super spy" by hiding whatever he's carrying inside his mouth and
suturing it to his forestomach or, through major surgery, placing it
deep in his stomach. The fourth and final way to use him is in a
tow system, with a ring over his nose such as you've seen at places

like Sea World and Marineland. Mr. Greenwood reminded his audience that the next Pearl Harbor could easily be a school of dolphins or killer whales carrying either deadly bacteria or hydrogen bombs.

Q. *Are sea otters still being hunted?* —M. O., EVERETT, OHIO

A. Not legally, but, because they seem to be increasing in numbers, the California Fish and Game Department is now not averse to the idea of starting the hunting again. The otters just barely escaped extinction, and have now managed to get a toe-hold in a small area off Monterey. The California Department of Fish and Game claims that they are "overpopulating their range"—meaning they are eating abalone that could go into commercial divers' bags. Forgotten is the fact that the otters' range once extended from the Bering Sea to Baja California, and the fact that otters and abalone coexisted abundantly for thousands of years. This is the same Fish and Game Department, you remember, that said it had to go on hunting mountain lions because it was the only way they could count them! "Cropping excess population," a California "outdoor" writer recently declared, "is sound wildlife management, and a dedicated hunter like the sea otter might be just the one to explain such a program to his protectors." No kidding, that's what the man said. We can see it now. A sea otter giving a speech to an animal welfare society and explaining why they should shoot him—for, of course, his own good.

Q. *This time I've got a question for you! What is one of the largest, most playful, friendliest, most communicative mammals there is—one that has a brain larger than man's and has many times rescued men in distress at sea—and yet is rewarded for all this by being imprisoned all alone, apparently, for life, in a basement of a hotel in a tub no larger than a fish tank?*

A. The answer is Doc, a dolphin. It's true. Since April of 1974, Doc has been imprisoned in the basement of the MGM Grand Hotel in Las Vegas. Since that time he has been used twice a night every night as a minor part of a long, boring spectacle show called "Halleluiah, Hollywood!"

Since Doc, who is twenty-two years old, antedates the Ocean Mammal Act, the MGM Grand people are not breaking any law— except the law of decency. They do know, however, that they are breaking that. They keep a tight security guard around Doc, allow no outsiders down to see him and do not even permit photos to be released at the Central News Bureau in Las Vegas.

According to a guard, "They used to transfer Doc to a bigger tank every night, but it got to be too much trouble." The same guard pointed to another tank. "They keep another dolphin, too," he said, "in case Doc gets sick. Her name is Lorelei. They can't let them see each other. If Doc knew Lorelei was there, he'd try to jump out of his tank into hers, and we'd all be in a lot of trouble."

Something can be done about Doc—and you can do it. Write to Kirk Kerkorian, Chairman of the Board, MGM Enterprises, Culver City, California 90230, and tell him this is one MGM enterprise you think he should end right now.

Q. *Have you ever seen Buffo, Oklahoma's famous stuffed buffalo? It is the most incredibly awful animal exhibit I ever saw.* —F. B., VICKSBURG, MICH.

A. I haven't seen it, but I read about it in *The Buffalo Book*, by David Dary—and I'm still reeling. Buffo, once a real buffalo, stands—stuffed—outside a wildlife preserve near Bartlesville. He acts—now get this—as a trash container. Litter placed in his mouth is carried in a long vacuum pipe through his body and into an adjacent room, where it drops into large containers; and "the vacuum," we are told, "is maintained at a level sufficient to transport empty beverage cans." Besides all this, Buffo talks—in, of course, deep buffalo tones. First he thanks children and other preserve visitors for not littering. Then he renders what is called "Buffo's Ode to All Buffalo"—a capsule history of the buffalo. Finally, he breaks into song. What does he sing? Right. "Home on the Range." Ain't man grand? At last we have a use for the buffalo:

a fun dispose-all. Like the fun man had, of course, disposing of them to begin with.

Q. *I read about birds being air-lifted during their winter migrations in Europe. I didn't know Europeans did anything to help birds.* —A. C., GASTONIA, N.C.

A. These Europeans did—perhaps because the birds had the luck to put down in Switzerland. What happened was that the myriad migrating swallows, on their way to Italy, southern France and Spain, were faced with an early and unseasonably cold winter that reduced the insect supply on which they feed during their migration.

They were not only cold, but starving, also. Whereupon practically everyone in Switzerland went to work—airlines, railroads, ornithological stations and bird protection societies, not to mention hundreds of policemen and firemen and thousands of schoolchildren and other volunteers. They collected the birds and brought them—by train, private car and even in makeshift cages strapped onto children's bicycles—to Swissair's cargo terminals at Zurich, Basel and Geneva. The first job, before they could be flown to Nice, Marseilles, Barcelona, Málaga, Casablanca, Athens, and so on, was to feed them. The job entailed hand-feeding little pieces of ground meat speared on matchsticks, and the toughest part of it was prying open the beaks. In other words, getting the swallows to swallow. But it was one animal story that was almost a total success—over one hundred thousand birds were saved. Wouldn't it be nice if the U.S. Army could solve some of its blackbird problems this way?

Q. *Was that story true about an elevated deer-crossing over the highway out West?* —E. P., DARLINGTON, S.C.

A. It was indeed. At least, it's planned—in Beaver, Utah. It's to be an overpass above the freeway, complete with fencing on it, as well as leading to and from it. It's also to be planted with enticing artificial vegetation. In five months, on that one freeway, sixty-seven deer were killed. Other states, and for that matter other countries, have built highway underpasses, but this is the first time I've heard of an overpass.

And, if you'll pardon the expression, it's high time. The fencing alongside our freeways, highways and parkways is woefully inadequate. Pennsylvania has found that deer will jump even seven-foot fences. Now they're planning nine-footers.

Did you know that tens of thousands of deer are killed each year on the highways? For once, animal people and hunters are on the same side of the fence—even if for different reasons. Even hunters, it seems, don't like the slogan, I Got My Buck with a Buick. On the other hand, there was a hunter in Vermont who saw something brown, fired off his 12-gauge shotgun, and tore the top off a convertible. And he couldn't tell anyone he thought it was a deer, either. You see, it was his convertible.

Q. *Is it true you said rodeos ought to be abolished?* —s. w., po-mona, calif.

A. No, I said rodeos ought to clean themselves up where cruelty is concerned. The Rodeo Cowboys Association and the International Rodeo Association are forever talking about policing their rodeos, but both of them together have authority over less than thirty percent of all rodeos. Hundreds upon hundreds of rodeos take place every year with no supervision at all. And the humane societies can't take any bows in this field either. They supervise fewer than ten percent of them. As for the rodeos that are "policed" . . . well, try for size this rule of the Rodeo Cowboys Association: "The placing of fingers in eyes, lips or nose of steers while wrestling is forbidden." Or try this one: "Standard electric prods shall be used as little as possible." That's some rule, all right. I'd call it a rule of thumb. To go, perhaps, with the fingers.

Or try this one—a report from the Fund for Animals' field agent, Sandy Rowland:

There are three of us, Larry Miller, Paul Hibler, and me, who will never forget the second horse to come out of the chute in the bucking event at the "Diamond S" Rodeo here. She got about fifteen feet into the ring, then, in an apparent frenzy to free herself from the bucking strap, she kicked her hindquarters up so high that she flipped over and fell. Up again, by now totally crazed, her saddle hanging on her underbelly and the bucking strap dangling, she smashed through the fence, charged through a tarp and bolted frantically behind the rodeo arena. Finally, she tripped on the bucking strap and fell once more. By now she had cuts all over her body and particularly on her face. The rodeo staff attempted to treat these with an aerosol spray. However, when they sprayed her face, I protested. It was obviously getting into her eye. The horse's owner reassured me. "Don't worry about that," he laughed. "She's blind in that eye."

The bucking strap is against the law in Ohio, and I am glad to report the owner was not only arrested and jailed, but had to put up a $1,000 bond. I am not so glad to report, however, that he jumped the bond, left town, and still has the horse. Watch for him. We'll get him—and the "Diamond S."

Q. *Why do we read about so many horses starving all over the place? What's the matter with people?* —E. M., DOVER, OHIO

A. The notorious Minnesota starvation case was infuriating enough. Particularly since that man who left the horses out (127 died), in the worst storm of the century in Minnesota, had been prosecuted for starving horses before. In my opinion, when a man is convicted of such a heinous crime he should never be permitted to own animals again. As for the notorious California case, this one is totally infuriating. It took place on the Chino, California, ranch of Rex Ellsworth, owner of the late, great Swaps. Swaps's own mother, as a matter of fact, was one of the brood mares who died from starvation. Four other mares were also dead, and four more aborted. How could a man like Ellsworth, who made a million dollars on Swaps alone, ever have allowed his ranch to descend to such horror? The answer isn't too hard to come by. One day, not long after Swaps had had a leg injury, and for weeks had been sus- pended in a sling, Ellsworth took two visitors to see him. Swaps was out of his sling, all right, but the visitors noted the stall was filthy. When Ellsworth turned on the overhead light, Swaps backed off at the sight of the strangers. Immediately Ellsworth grabbed him by the mane and then, incredibly, punched him hard in the middle of his face. "That will teach you," he said, "to mind your manners."

Maybe it's time someone taught Ellsworth not only manners but also humanity—and in the same way.

Q. *My nephew got the most awful, violence-inspiring toy for Christmas. Can't something be done about this form of inhumane education?*
—P. T., WESTLAND, MICH.

A. Well, we're trying, but it is discouraging, every Christmas holiday, to see the vast array of toys having to do with shooting, killing and general violence with which we choose to celebrate peace on earth. My least favorite this year is a thing called Rabbit Hunt. It consists of a toy double-barreled shotgun, a mechanical rabbit and darts with rubber suction tips. Such toys are not only physically dangerous to children, they can be psychologically damaging as well. If any child you know is playing with one of these horrors, try to convince the parents to have it exchanged for something the child can really grow with.

Q. *In your book,* Man Kind? *you implied that there are no rules in the woods and that hunters, as members of Conservation and Fish and Game Departments, are, as you put it, "judge and jury." For your edification, each year the Pennsylvania Game Commission publishes a book of almost two hundred pages of rules.* —C. P., LIGONIER, PA.

A. I read your Pennsylvania Game Law book. Whoever decreed that animals were "game"? I also saw the opening note: "SPORTS-MEN'S DOLLARS USED FOR PUBLICATION OF THIS BOOK." It seemed, if you will pardon the expression, that they gave the game away with that one. Anyway, it's some book, all right—just about what I would expect from a state that gives its gunmen not only the right to kill virtually anything that moves (and has bounties on a wide variety of animals), but also the right to kill people. Yes, people.

If you don't believe it, try Section 825. It's called "Shooting at Human Beings in Mistake." Lovely title, what? Actually, it goes on: it tells you it is "unlawful to shoot at human beings in mistake" and, we quote, "while actually shooting at any game or wild creature." Under subdivision A of Section 825 the book tells us that if you do shoot at humans but don't injure them, it will cost you "not less than $100 nor more than $300."

On the other hand, if you injure a human, it will cost you "not less than $200 nor more than $500." Our favorite though, is subdivision C, which is entitled "Killing Human Beings in Mistake." If you do that, the book tells you, it will cost you (and again we quote) "for the first offense" (honestly, that's what it says) "not less than $500 nor more than $1,000." And this amount, the book concludes, you pay to "the personal representative of the deceased."

Q. *The damn hunting season is on us up here—first "early bear," then "bow," then the bang-bang, slaughter-slaughter, on and on. Isn't anything ever going to be done about it?* —B. R., SILVERNAILS, N.Y.

A. Cheer up—and duck. Speaking of ducks, maybe this little story will give you heart. It comes from Dr. Arthur Peterson of DeBary, Florida, who has a lake down there with both domesticated and migratory ducks. A while back he noticed some strange goings-on between two of them. Although it was not mating season, John-Duck, as he called one, was amazingly attentive to Mary-Duck, as he called the other. He was always with her and incredibly protective of her. If Dr. Peterson or anybody else came near, John-Duck would quack loudly and even nudge Mary-Duck to safety. Finally, one day Dr. Peterson surprised Mary-Duck alone. He slipped a net over her and examined her. Mary-Duck was totally blind! Dr. Peterson, of course, immediately released her. And sure enough, faithful John-Duck at once reappeared, gave a reassuring quack and once more guided her off. What next—guide ducks for the blind?

Q. *Is it true Princeton University sent out a letter against hunting?* —C. K., BOSTON, MASS.

A. No, but the Institute for Advanced Study in Princeton, New Jersey, did—addressed to Members Resident in the Housing Project. It was entitled "Safety in The Woods," and it read as follows:

> *The hunting season in The State of New Jersey runs from October 6 to February 2.*
>
> *Although Princeton Township has adopted an ordinance prohibiting the discharge of firearms within the township boundaries and we post the institute lands against all types of hunting and employ a game warden during the entire hunting season, the perimeter of the institute property is so long that it is impossible to keep every hunter from neighboring townships from entering the institute woods.*
>
> *Members and their families are urged to use extreme caution while walking in the woods during the hunting season and to refrain from walking in the woods during the December deer season unless they are dressed in very bright attire. Unattended children will not be entirely safe at any time, and they should be forbidden to enter the woods at all in December.*

This memo came to my attention after my book *Man Kind?* had gone to press. It's too bad. It says it all: a handful of gunmen are able to make the woods unsafe for the rest of us, even though we outnumber them ten to one.

Q. *What do you think of the famous "one-shot" antelope hunt in Colorado?* —S. F., CHICAGO, ILL.

A. I think it's awful. The sad part is that—as in the case of the bow-and-arrow hunt and other misguided efforts to give the animal a better chance and more even odds and all that sort of thing—this kind of hunt actually ends up being more cruel.

It is held not in Colorado, but in Lander, Wyoming, each September. The governors of Colorado and Wyoming invite all the other Western governors to form teams of three; then famous hunters form teams of three, and there is also a celebrity team.

There's a big evening of drinking and old-fashioned Western "pleasures" the night before; then, at five-thirty in the morning the teams are routed out of bed and each member is given one bullet. The team which kills the largest number of antelopes with its total of three bullets—obviously, the maximum kill is three—wins. If there is a tie, as happened last fall, when both the Colorado and the Nevada teams got two antelopes, then the team which got its kill first wins. With three bullets, what team is going to waste one on a wounded animal?

And there's the rub—how the animal is killed. The hunters carry knives, but on one hunt a governor who shall be nameless was seen beating a wounded antelope to death with a rock.

Incidentally, before the hunt begins the people are asked not to emulate the late actor Jack Carson, who was once a member of the celebrity team. Carson had quite an evening the night before, and was awakened only with greatest difficulty the next morning. Finally, though, he was on his way with his bullet. When he got into the center of town, he suddenly grabbed his gun and fired the bullet at the sky. "Tell the rest of the sons of bitches I missed," Carson said, "I'm going back to bed."

Q. *I've been hearing about the overpopulation of domestic animals for years, but now I'm beginning to hear about the overpopulation of zoo animals. You mean they can't control the birth rate of animals in zoos? Come on!* —R. A., BOSTON, MASS.

A. It's true; in some zoos the situation has passed from being a nuisance to being serious. Last year, for example, the Denver zoo experienced such success with its breeding program for lions that it looked for a while as if four of their newest cubs were going to have to be killed before they got a toehold on life at all.

In many cases the overpopulation of a certain species in a certain zoo is due to unexpected success in that zoo's breeding program. But in other cases it can just be a matter of old and outdated facilities not being able to accommodate any newcomers at all.

In her marvelous book *A Bird in the Bush and a Bear in the Hand*, West Coast humanitarian Judy Hughes tells of rescuing many surplus animals from zoos to live at her unique halfway-house ranch in Oregon.

Among the animals Mrs. Hughes acquired was a bear cub from a small local zoo where, she writes, the bear had been confined in a cage so small that it could neither stand up nor move about, but only rock back and forth.

When finally released into her care the bear was so overjoyed that, Mrs. Hughes recalls, it got into the car, blew the horn, turned on the headlights and the windshield wiper, and finally, in a burst of happiness, even turned on the radio.

Q. *I've heard you have a wonderful name for outdoor writers.* —S. M., VERONA, N.J.

A. I've called them various names, but my favorite is the name given them by the famous Los Angeles radio and TV personality, Michael Jackson—"Frosty Numbfingers."

Q. *Is there really any proof that people who later become criminals mistreated animals as children?* —A. M., VALDOSTA, GA.

A. There is proof aplenty—and from all over. The latest is in *Ogonyok*, a Soviet magazine. It reported on an examination of a wide variety of criminals, including robbers and rapists. Out of 135 of these, it stated, 118 admitted that when they were young they burned, hanged or stabbed domestic animals.

Q. *What, in your opinion, is the most prevalent cruelty perpetrated on dogs and cats?* —F. J., BLOOMFIELD HILLS, MICH.

A. To my mind the most prevalent cruelty is, simply, ignoring them. Dogs or cats, like children, have to belong. They are not things—they are living beings. If they aren't really loved, at least they must feel important. I've been in so many homes where the dog or the cat is just there, but that's all. He or she has no real master or mistress, and his or her life is a miserable mixture of boredom, frustration and loneliness. A cat particularly may not seem to want or even need attention—but it does. The chances are the animal has retreated into that position because it just didn't get any.

I just visited the campus of Hampshire College in Amherst, Massachussetts. I saw many animals on campus, but the happiest were the ones which were both loved and had jobs to do, too. I remember one particular German shepherd. His young master hadn't given him any real job, so he made up his own. And you know what it was? It was to break up fights among other animals. Whenever he heard real barking or growling, he'd go tearing over to break it up. He was really something, that dog. Something important.

Q. *I heard about the pig that was swimming in the middle of the ocean and was rescued by a Florida fisherman. The next thing I knew, the pig was shot. Why?* —K. A., NORTH BRANCH, N.J.

A. A good question. I talked with the fisherman. His name is Mike Leadley, of Hialeah. He was out in a sports fishing boat with three pals, one of whom is a Cuban jockey. The jockey went to sleep, and, to play a joke on him, the others decided to go far out and pretend, when he woke up, that they were lost. But the joke never came off. Because they suddenly saw, swimming out there fifteen miles off shore in the middle of nowhere, what they first thought was a shark. The pig was almost completely exhausted, swimming over on his side, but when he saw the boat, he squealed and made for it. The men pulled Porketariat, as someone called him, in, gave him water and doughnuts, and found him to be both grateful and affectionate. On the way back they hailed another boat—"to have a witness," Leadley told me. "I still didn't believe it." Once they got the pig ashore and housed in a shack behind Leadley's house, they set about getting a home for him—and, in fact, had a definite home with a woman who ran a country school for retarded children.

At this point, a man from the U.S. Department of Agriculture arrived on the scene, took "the hog," as he called it, to the Miami Airport Quarantine Station, and killed it. "He was a real pet," Leadley told me. "I didn't like the cut-and-dried way the man took him. There were ways to quarantine him and still save him. If they could have seen the way that pig was pleading to come aboard that boat, they would never have killed him."

I agree. I have also talked with virtually all the Florida and Washington departments of agriculture people in charge, and while I admit there must be protection against livestock diseases, I am still curious what diseases that particular pig—which had almost certainly been outward-bound on a ship headed for the islands—could have brought in that could not be brought in by the thousands and thousands of small laboratory pigs (not guinea pigs) annually imported for research purposes. The idea that that pig would be carrying African swine fever and hence would have swum, by that reasoning, from Africa, I find preposterous. One Department of Agriculture spokesman told a protester, "We simply didn't know enough about its background." To which my reply was, "I doubt if the pig had wanted to be a debutante."

Q. *Please, please write about that beaver Chopper.* —S. R., BOWL-ING GREEN, OHIO.

A. I'll do better than that. I'll quote you a letter I received about him from Karyl Carter, a Girl Scout:

> *A beaver who swam, dove and somersaulted among canoeing Girl Scouts—that's the sight you would have seen at Camp Sacajawea Girl Scout Camp in Newfield, New Jersey, this summer.*
> *It was a late-morning discovery. Girls from Holly Shores Girl Scout Council were taking canoeing lessons in Sacy's Lake when a large stump started to move and perform numerous swimming feats. Hearing laughter, squeals and screams, the waterfront director canoed out to the girls, identified the stump as a* real *beaver and yelled to those on the beach, "Go get the rest of the camp . . . they've never seen anything like this before." In no time flat, the entire camp lined*

the lakefront, playing audience to a most talented but different kind of swimmer.

The waterfront director, who was wary but excited, told the canoers, "Just keep canoeing, don't pet the beaver, but enjoy the experience." Meanwhile, a beach bystander ran to the camp office and called Hope Buyukmihci, naturalist and author, at Unexpected Wildlife Refuge, three miles away. "Are you missing a beaver . . . a very friendly one?" The answer was yes. The beaver was Chopper, an orphan Ms. Buyukmihci had raised from infancy, and he was now over a year old and beginning to make it on his own in the wild.

Minutes later, Hope drove in to Camp Sacy to con Chopper back home. But the next day Chopper was back in Sacy's Lake, entertaining campers with his swimabatics. "Maybe he's building a dam. Maybe he's going to raise a family," said some of his young admirers.

All of us were excited over these prospects. We told Hope about Chopper's whereabouts. She said he could stay and was happy that Chopper was on his own.

Every day, the staff members kept Hope informed of Chopper's activities. "He may try to climb into your boats," she said, "but he's just playing. He'll dive off immediately. And he might just swim along or wrestle with you if you're in the water!"

For the next three days, campers, leaders and staff members observed, petted, fed and just plain enjoyed Chopper. The Girl Scouts also learned about the looks, diet, habits and temperament of a beaver who is accustomed to the world of people.

During these beaver days, the atmosphere in the camp drastically changed. There was a profound awareness that there really was something alive and friendly out there in the woods and waters.

One afternoon the camp director decided to take some pictures of Chopper. He found him swimming in a swampy area near the Comanche campsite. An animal enthusiast, the director walked right into the swamp, click-clicked the camera and was then promptly but playfully grabbed around the leg by Chopper.

The following day was hectic, with camp closing and campers leaving. It wasn't until late Saturday afternoon that a few remaining staff members decided to walk down to the lake and say good-bye to Chopper.

As we approached the lakefront, there were other last-minute beaver admirers standing on the dock. They screamed, "Come quickly!" We ran, only to find Chopper lying on the edge of the dock—dead.

These people, many of whom were young campers, had just wit-nessed an unidentified fisherman maliciously beat Chopper to death. It seemed Chopper was disturbing this trespassing man's sport. The fish-erman, who was rowing away, shouted to us, "That thing tried to climb into my boat, so I hit it with my fishing pole. Then it started to hiss at me. I had to hit it with my oar."
We wrapped Chopper in a beach towel. We cried. . . .

Q. *I heard that a dog in a pound in the Midwest somewhere was first gassed and then shot and still wasn't killed. How can things like this hap-pen?* —A. D., KEENE, N.H.

A. They happen because, up to now at least, not enough peo-ple care. The dog to which you refer was picked up by a Salem, Ohio, dog warden and taken to a dump in a truck. He was gassed (with carbon monoxide) in a chamber in the truck. Forty-five min-utes later, another warden came along and found the dog still alive. The dog wouldn't come to him when he called him, so he shot him—four times. That warden then went away; later he explained that it was raining and he didn't want to get his shoes dirty. That night, James Gilbert, a bulldozer operator, found the dog in a shack, still alive, but with two gaping wounds—the bullets had en-tered his shoulder and gone out his chest. Gilbert called Mrs. Joyce Guiler and Miss Jean Fluharty, and Dumpy, as the women called him, recovered. They will never forget that when they picked him up he wagged his tail.

Unhappily, he has died—but not of the dog pound's gassing or of the warden shooting at him four times. He died, or rather had to be destroyed, because, as his heartbroken rescuer, Joyce Guiler, told me, "The person who had once owned him didn't have the sense to get him distemper shots." Dumpy is buried at the Wood-side Pet Cemetery in Navarre, Ohio. On his tombstone are the words, "We the People Will Never Forget You." But will we? And, speaking of dog pounds, what about cats? No county or city pound in Ohio handles cats. If you bring a cat or cats in a closed box to the warden, and don't open it, the warden will as a favor put the box down and shoot it full of holes. As a favor, mind you. In such a box how many are shot dead and how many half-dead?

Q. *Does anybody care about frogs?* —P. F., HINGHAM, MASS.

A. They ought to. They are subjected to every imaginable cruelty, not only via the eating of frogs' legs, but also for sport. Remember the famous line, "The boy kills the frog for sport, but the frog dies in earnest." And don't forget those grand frog-jumping contests—wonderful sport for the whole family. This spring, at the Sacramento Convention Hall, the Easter Seal Society put on a real dilly. "The children," one eyewitness reported, "attempted to make the frogs jump by throwing them to the ground and then stomping so close that sometimes they stomped on them. If the frogs still didn't jump, the children knelt down and blasted a horn in their ears."

Frogs are also subjected to unspeakable cruelties in biology classes. The famous pithing, for example, doesn't necessarily mean the frog is killed. Often he is dissected alive. One San Francisco Science Fair awarded a prize to a junio high student who cut the head off a frog with a pair of scissors, and then tried to make him swim. His findings for his paper: "Frogs will not swim with brain missing unless harassed. A frog swims better with head on."

Compare those stories to the story of the duke of Wellington, at the height of his fame in 1837, riding along and seeing, by the side of the road, a boy in great distress over his tame toad. He was going off to boarding school, he said, and no one would look after the toad. "Then," said the Iron Duke, "I will." And all the way through school, the boy received letters—one of which still exists. "Field Marshall the Duke of Wellington is happy to inform William Harris that his toad is alive and well."

That was in 1837. We've sure made a lot of progress, haven't we?

Q. *Did you by any chance hear what happened in Oklahoma when they introduced a bill banning cockfighting?* —B. A., MILLEDGEVILLE, GA.

A. I did indeed; in fact, the story was sent to me. When Representative Charles Prentice introduced his bill to outlaw cockfighting, the Oklahoma lawmakers not only thought very little of the idea but also declared it unpatriotic.

Representative John Monks said that cockfighting had a great history in the United States and that George Washington was a cockfight promoter. He also maintained that countries that had been great powers quickly declined after banning cockfights.

"Look at the British Empire," Monks roared. "When the empire was in its prime, Henry VIII had a royal cockfighting pit. Now," he said, "England has gone from a ferocious lion to a toothless pussycat."

Then Monks really warmed to his task. "In every country of the world taken over by the communists," he shouted, "one of the first things they do is to outlaw cockfighting."

Besides being incorrect, this was too much for the bill's author. He admitted that there may have been some early patriots who were cockfight promoters. But so, he declared, was Benedict Arnold.

Our favorite Oklahoma lawmaker, though, was a former sheriff, Representative George Vaughn. He somehow equated cockfighting with Women's Liberation—and opposed both. "God didn't make woman from the head of man," he declared, "so she could do the thinking."

Somehow it seems a pity the Deity didn't. Somebody down there should be doing the thinking—besides, that is, the people elected to do so.

Q. *What is cruel about dog racing?* —R. A., ENGLEWOOD, FLA.

A. Just about everything. Take, for openers, the way the greyhounds are trained. They don't run after a live rabbit on the track; it is a mechanical rabbit. But to train them to run after it—to think it is a live rabbit—involves—you guessed it—live rabbits. And the first step in this training is to teach the greyhound to kill.

Take this report from John Burns, of the Tarrant County (Texas) Humane Society.

In the south part of Tarrant County, on every clear Sunday, wild rabbits captured in the deserts of New Mexico and west Texas huddle in a pen in an enclosed field. Large crowds of people—men, women and children—gather for an afternoon of "fun."

The fun consists of watching these rabbits released from the pen, one by one, to be chased by greyhounds across the field. There is no escape for the rabbits. The field is fenced. The fastest dog rips the rabbit apart while the spectators watch excitedly. Some races end in a draw. That means that two or even three dogs simultaneously tear the rabbit apart. Few of the kills are clean. The screams of the rabbit sometimes last an entire minute.

Some rabbits die before the dogs reach them; they go berserk with fear and kill themselves as they hurl themselves against the fence.

Families with children attend these races. To them, it is a Sunday outing. Those who defend this cruelty say, "What does it matter? They are only rabbits!"

Texas state law does not protect these rabbits. The law states (1) that a person cannot injure or kill an animal belonging to another, and (2) that animals cannot be made to fight each other. According to our district attorney, the owner of the greyhound track is not guilty of cruelty for two reasons: (1) he owns the rabbits, and (2) the dog and the rabbit cannot be said to be fighting each other because the rabbit does not fight back.

Fight *back!* Isn't that lovely. But at Moose Martin's training track, even that isn't enough. Young greyhounds apparently get discouraged if they can't get a rabbit quickly, so the trainers obligingly break one of the rabbit's front legs. But this is just the *first* step. After the greyhounds get their taste for rabbit, then comes the second stage in the training.

For this, there is what is called a "schooling" track. First a live rabbit, head down, dangling inches off the ground, is tied to the lure by its back legs. This lure is slowed as the dogs approach the finish line. The dogs are allowed one bite, and then the rabbit, still alive, is speeded up again.

Even after this training, it's still a horrible "sport." Recent studies indicate that for the average dog-racing track, approximately 2,100 greyhounds between two and three years of age are killed annually. These are dogs that were not fast enough to win, and hence are purposely killed. When puppies and older dogs killed are added to these figures, the number goes up to 2,500 a year. And that, mind you, is for *each* track.

Q. *I understand that the real reason Ruffian died is that fundamental thing wrong with horseracing: the racing of two-year-olds. Is this true?*
—W. J., RALEIGH, N.C.

A. Yes—and no. Horses are raced when they are too young. The so-called two-year-old is often not a two-year-old. All horses are given January birthdates and, conceivably, a horse foaled on New Year's Eve would be a "two-year-old" at the age of one year and one day. This doesn't often happen, but many, many horses are foaled in May and June and are heavily raced at a year and a half, when their physical development and their bones are not mature.

Some years ago the Jockey Club appointed a special veterinarian panel to study the problem and, ironically, two of its members were Dr. William O. Reed, who operated on Ruffian, and Dr. Manual A. Gilman, who made Ruffian's diagnosis.

This panel instituted a program at the New York tracks and Santa Anita and Hollywood Park, in which a two-year-old could be X-rayed free of charge. Almost a quarter of them were found to be horses that should have been, in the veterinarians' words, "either put on very slow training or taken out of training entirely."

"We believe that an immature two-year-old cannot possibly do the work required of a mature horse," said Dr. Gilman. "This is as true for a two-year-old horse as it would be for a sixteen-year-old boy playing football with the New York Giants. Everyone would have to agree that he would be more prone to injury than his teammates would, no matter how good a football player he was."

Nothing was done after this report, of course, which is all too typical of horse racing. Even the cruel Romans, who used a definitely stronger horse than today's thoroughbred in their chariot races, never "broke" their horses until they were actual three-year-olds and didn't race them until they were five. Incidentally, vet-

erinarians agree that five is the age when the animal is an adult—
meaning completely developed.

Although Ruffian had had a fracture before the match race—
one that kept her out of the Kentucky Derby—she had not been
heavily raced as a two-year-old. But she was still a very young
horse, the track was hard and the competition was terrific. Dr.
Reed told me, "I think we should be more cautious about racing
two-year-olds. And I am definitely inclined to disfavor the racing
of two-year-olds until they really are two-year-olds.

"With Ruffian," Dr. Reed added, "you had a horse that had
terrific speed, and there was an explosive effect on her legs and
ankles because of that speed. It wasn't so much the pounding on
the track; it was just the speed.

"Remember Harry ('the Cat') Brecheen, the baseball pitcher?
He had terrific speed, and he broke his arm just by pitching. Yet
he was able to come back after an operation.

"The really sad thing about Ruffian was that she was in such
awful condition to be operated on. She came off such a terrible,
stressful situation. There was such incredible sweating, even at
eight o'clock, when we started to operate—such a loss of fluids.
She was in shock. Her heartbeat was 76; it should have been 36.

"The biggest problem was just stabilizing her as a patient on
the table. The ideal situation would have been to operate when the
horse was completely stable. We couldn't wait because of the con-
tamination of the leg from the injury and other factors involved."

Q. *If you wrote an epitaph for Ruffian, what would it be?* —E. D.,
ELMONT, N.Y.

A. One that I liked was sent to me by D. Vivian Youngman of
Tampa, Forida. It goes as follows:

Here lies a testament to man's greed;
Of those who bet, and of those who breed.
A dustless, short flash across the sky,
And this gorgeous filly had to die.

The End of the Tail

America is a strange country, as far as animals are concerned. I am indebted to Barry Cornet of New York for pointing out some strange animal laws. They are all on the books; indeed, they are *in* a book by Barbara Seuling called *You Can't Eat Peanuts in Church, and Other Little-Known Laws*.

In Reed City, Michigan, it is illegal to own a cat and a bird.

In Wyoming, it is illegal to take a picture of a rabbit during January, February, March or April—unless you have a license.

In the state of Washington, it is illegal to hunt ducks from a rowboat unless you are upright and visible from the waist up.

Several states—California, Oklahoma, Idaho and North Dakota—prohibit the trapping of birds in cemeteries.

In California, picking feathers from a live goose is illegal.

In Knoxville, Tennessee, it is illegal to lasso a fish.

In Boston, it was once illegal to own a dog more than ten inches high.

In Boston, too, a hotel owner is still required by law to put up and bed down a guest's horse.

According to an old law in Truro, Massachusetts, a young

man could not get married until he had killed either six blackbirds or three crows.

In Denver, the law insists that dog-catchers notify dogs of impounding by posting a notice on a tree in the park.

In Topeka, Kansas, it is illegal to worry a squirrel.

In Arizona, it is a crime to kick a mule.

In Little Rock, Arkansas, dogs are not allowed to bark after six P.M.

In Paulding, Ohio, it is legally proper for a policeman to bite a barking dog to quiet him.

In Baltimore, it is against the law to mistreat an oyster.

In the state of Illinois, an animal can be sent to jail.

In San Antonio, Texas, it is illegal for monkeys to ride buses.

In Washington, D.C., you are prohibited from punching a bull on the nose.

In Berea, Ohio, an animal on the street after dark must display a red taillight.

In Alderson, West Virginia, lions are not permitted to run wild in the streets.

In Quitman, Georgia, it is illegal for a chicken to cross the road.

In Connecticut, the law states that if you are a beaver, you have a legal right to build a dam.

But my favorite of all is a Kentucky statute: "No female shall appear in a bathing suit on any highway within this state unless she is escorted. . . ." A subsequent amendment to this statute reads: "The provisions of this statute shall not apply to females weighing less than ninety pounds nor more than two hundred pounds, nor shall it apply to female horses."

Who said our laws didn't think of *everything?*

Q. *I read somewhere that some day we'll all have animal servants doing our housework. Did I dream it?* —L. J., KENNEBUNKPORT, MAINE

A. Unfortunately you didn't—but maybe you should have. In any case, it would be a bad dream—just like the old days when

dogs went around and around all day in basements, operating treadmills. What you heard about was a symposium at the London zoo at which Dr. Boris Levinson, professor emeritus of psychology and author of *Pet-Oriented Child Psychotherapy*, declared that in twenty-five years man would have animals completely controlled by electrodes. "In a sense," he said, "the electrodes will make the animals become living robots. They will be able, at the turn of a dial, to open doors, close windows, make beds, et cetera." Later Dr. Levinson also told a reporter, "We can already plant minute electrodes into animals' brains to make them placid, angry or to stop them attacking. It is only a matter of time before they can be implanted into every part of the brain, to make the animals do whatever we wish."

Q. *I get so sick of people saying, about someone bad, "He's an animal." The other day, for example, right after that horrible mass murder in Connecticut, one of the policemen was quoted as saying the murderer had to be "an animal." What can I do about it?* —B. L., GLEN BURNIE, MD.

A. Write to the person or to the TV or radio show where you hear such a remark. My book, *Man Kind?* starts with a discussion of our strange language put-downs. We even call each other animal names—"You pig," "you swine," "you rat," "you skunk," "you baboon," or "you jackal." And we do it in the hope, of course, that as we do it we don't make too much of a "jackass," or perhaps just "an ass" out of ourselves. The second dictionary definition of *coyote* is "a contemptible sneak," of *bear*, "a clumsy, ill-mannered person."

And how many of our similes are unfavorably animal-oriented? For every brave as a lion, busy as a beaver or even wise as an owl or cute as a bug, there are literally dozens of cross as a bear, mean as a snake, sly as a fox, dumb as an ox, slippery as an eel, stubborn as a mule, silly as a goose, crazy as a loon, greedy as a pig and so on. You may cry crocodile tears, but if you're hurt, you'll squeal like a stuck pig. You may be hogtied, but it depends on whose ox is being gored. We may put on the dog, but more likely someone treats you like a dog. You may go to the dogs, or something may happen to you that shouldn't happen to a dog. And, finally, in election week, what do we say about a politician we despise? We say he couldn't get elected dog-catcher.

You badger someone; someone in turn buffaloes you. You're either chicken or sheepish or you toady to someone, or you go ape. You're bull-headed or a dumb bunny or mousy. You have bats in your belfry or you're batty or you're up to monkey business. If something is wrong, there's something fishy. We have even named one of the seven deadly sins after one animal, the lovable sloth.

A man is either a wolf (who will, of course, turn) or else he's an old goat; a woman can look like a horse, or be horse-faced, or, worse still, a cow. She can also be a shrew or a vixen. And, last but not least, we come to the animals closest to us of all—the cat and the dog. And we have words for them galore, all the way from our worst stocks—even stock-market officials refer to them as cats and dogs—to our lowest form of living—which would either be in the doghouse or, horror of horrors, the cathouse.

And what are we when we're catty? Why, obviously, we're mean. And if a woman is unattractive, what is she? Why, a dog. Someone is nervous as a cat or a fraidy cat. Someone else lets the cat out of the bag. Still a third person declares, "There are more ways than one to skin a cat."

Q. *What do you say when someone still uses that old argument that animals have no souls?* —N. J., TORONTO, ONT.

A. I say if it's true that animals have no souls and that if we're all going to some wonderful Elysian Fields and they're not, then that is all the more reason to give them a better shake in the one life they do have.

Q. *Why don't schools teach humane education?* —H. M., WINAMAC, IND.

A. The best answer to this question, to my mind, was made by Richard Calore, a man who personally presents programs of humane education to more than 250,000 boys and girls each year. Education, he points out, is the country's largest enterprise. It is the occupation of more than 63 million men, women and children. Of this total, 60 million are students and 3 million are teachers, and last year, according to the U.S. Office of Education, 90 billion dollars were spent by school systems and educational institutitons. And how much of this was spent teaching children to be kind to their fellow creatures? Actually, specifically, not a dime.

Q. *I keep reading awful things about animals in reference books and children's books—old-fashioned, antianimal statements that have been thoroughly disproved. What can I do?* —R. N., SULPHUR, OKLA.

A. The best thing you can do is to write to me with the specific instance. In fairness, reference and children's books are trying to be better about these old wives' tales, but it will take time. Remember, animals have been put down for centuries. I agree with you, it's infuriating. In the same mail in which I received your letter, for example, I received one from Norma Eason of Frankfort, Michigan, who wrote me about a social studies book that her third-grade son had brought home. It was published by the Hayes School Publishing Company of Wilkinsburg, Pennsylvania, and here's what it said about the wolf:

> *The gray wolf or timber wolf is the largest member of the dog family in North America. Wolves kill so many farm animals that state governments used to give prizes for shooting them. Wolves cannot be tamed enough to become pets. They are cruel. If one wolf gets hurt, other wolves will eat him. One wolf had lived in a cage with his mate for a year, and then he killed her and ate her. Wolves will not even fight for their cubs. There are not so many wolves in America as there used to be.*

If that isn't bad enough, next try what the book said about wolverines:

> *The wolverine is about the size of a bulldog. Its body and legs are thick and strong. It is a great thief. It takes things from trappers'*

cabins it cannot use in any way. It goes to the traps and eats what he has caught and sometimes goes off with the traps. It is the only animal we know of that destroys property just because he enjoys it. It lives in the northern part of the Rocky Mountains. There are a great many in Alaska.

Isn't that just awful, though? An animal who takes things from trappers' cabins that he cannot use in any way. Like, we presume, a spare wolverine?

Q. *Have you ever read "Why Some People Don't Like Dogs and Why Other People Like Dogs"?* —K. B., LAKE STEVENS, WASH.

A. Yes, I have. It is in *The Dog's Scrapbook*, albeit anonymously. For those of you who haven't read it, here it is:

WHY SOME PEOPLE DON'T LIKE DOGS
They follow their owners everywhere.
They stick their cold noses into one's hand at unexpected moments.
They always want to play.
They jump up on their friends and lick them to show their affection.

WHY OTHER PEOPLE LIKE DOGS
They follow their owners everywhere.
They stick their cold noses into one's hand at unexpected moments.
They always want to play.
They jump up on their friends and lick them to show their affection.

Q. *People who write about dogs are always writing about* French *poodles,* German *shepherds,* English *bulldogs. Aren't there any* American *dogs?* —R. J., STONYBROOK, L. I.

A. There are indeed. Perhaps the most famous of America's own dogs—and a dog which has become legendary—is the Newfoundland. Although he comes from that island that gave him his name, he is descended from the now extinct "American" black wolf, and was domesticated by the Algonquins and the Sioux. (Foreign breeders used to argue that the Newfoundland couldn't be American; he was too loyal, majestic and intelligent to have been bred by savages!) George Washington, Samuel Adams, and Benjamin Franklin all owned Newfoundlands and soon they were popular in other countries. Queen Victoria had a Newfoundland; so did the painter, Edwin Landseer. In fact, it was Landseer who made popular the black-and-white (or Landseer) Newfoundland, rather than the all-black. (One way he did it was simple: When he painted a portrait of somebody with an all-black Newfoundland, he painted the dog black and white anyway.)

The Newfoundland has left some indelible marks on history. The rescues made by Newfoundlands have, of course, been legendary. One Newfoundland alone saved ninety passengers and crew during a blizzard off the coast of Newfoundland. Napoleon himself owed his life to a Newfoundland. Leaving Elba on a dark and stormy night for his "One Hundred Days," the Emperor slipped and fell off a rock and could not be quickly located by his aides. Never a swimmer, and having grown fat and weak as a prisoner, he would have drowned had not a Newfoundland belonging to the boatswain jumped into the water and, just as he was sinking, grabbed him and towed him to the boat.

Byron's dog, Boatswain, is probably the best known of all Newfoundlands—immortalized by the poet's own tribute to one who "Possesses Beauty without Vanity, Strength without Insolence, Courage without Ferocity, and all Virtues of Man without his Vices." But there are many great Newfoundlands. "Scannon," for example, the Newfoundland owned by Captain Lewis of Lewis and Clark, was such an incredible dog that at the start of one difficult winter, Lewis wrote in his journal that other than Clark, he was sure of only one member of the expedition—Scannon.

Still another famous Newfoundland was "Major," who was

not only the mascot of the famed "Tenth Maine" in the Civil War, but who actually fought with his regiment. Once captured, he refused steadfastly to make friends with any Confederates, soon escaped and was back with his side in the first wave of attacks at both Antietam and Cedar Mountain. In both these battles, historian Margaret Booth Chern recalls, "He bit all the Confederates he could." Later, at the Battle of Mansfield, in Louisiana, he was shot through the head and killed.

In recent times, the most famous Newfoundland was, of course, Brumis, the great dog of the late Robert Kennedy. On one occasion, at the swearing in of N. A. Schlei as Assistant Attorney General, it is recorded that just as Justice John Marshall Harlan held out the Bible for Schlei to swear upon, Brumis jumped up, pushed Justice Harlan aside, put his great paws on Schlei's shoulders and earnestly searched his face before allowing the Justice to proceed with the oath.

Q. *I know its not Christmas, but would you tell that sad and touching story of* The Christmas Pup? —A. D., BAYVILLE, N.Y.

A. Indeed I will. Written over half a century ago by that great animal writer, Albert Payson Terhune, *The Christmas Pup* is today as tragically true as it ever was. It goes, in part, like this:

> *Up to the preceding day, the baby collie had lived cozily in the puppy yard at his breeder's farm, along with his gentle mother and his three brothers and sisters. It had been a peaceful and jolly life. From humans he had known nothing but friendliness. The world, to him, was a wondrous nice place to live in; a friendly and amusing place.*
>
> *Then he had been put into a crate and sent in a bewildering long and jolting train trip that had lasted for a whole day. Still his faith in the friendliness of the world had not wavered, nor had his gay courage been shaken. From the train the crate had been loaded on a truck and presently he had been lifted out at this strange and brightly lit house and had been tied to a chair in a strange and brightly lit room and left there alone—he who had never before been in a house or had been awake at such a late hour.*
>
> *It had not occurred to anyone that he might be dead-tired from his long journey or that he might be half-starved or suffering from*

*thirst—as he was—or that rest and quiet are the first and greatest needs
of a puppy on reaching a new home. But he was a gallant little chap
and eager for new, happy adventure. So he did not cry or give other
sign of his growing physical malaise. Then to him avalanched a mob of
young humans who caught him up and pulled him about and yelled to
him and, in their grabbings, bruised his pudgily tender little body. It
was a bedlam of noise and rough handling and of slowly dawning terror for the gently reared puppy.*

*The parents beamed fondly on the pretty sight. They were pleased
they had made their children so happy by this expensive gift.*

*The puppy whimpered as one child yanked him away from an-
other. There was a roar of laughter as someone suggested the little
collie was trying to sing. To cause an "encore" of the "song," the oldest
girl tweaked his tail.*

*Panic and pain had begun to replace the puppy's first gladness of
meeting these new humans. Panic and pain and bewilderment. The
sharp tug at his sensitive tail completed the wreck of his highstrung
nerves. Not knowing what he did, he turned and snapped, in feeble
protest, at the torturing hand. One milk tooth scratched lightly the
skin of the girl's thumb. At once her father strode forward, snatched
the puppy from his precious daughter and struck him heavily over the
head; then kicked him into a corner.*

*"They've sent me a vicious dog, the crooks!" he thundered, while
his wife stooped to kiss the abraded thumb. "The filthy brute has
hydrophobia! Look at him!"*

*The puppy was lying in a quivering heap in the corner, whither
he had been kicked. Foam was flecking his mouth; his eyes were rolling. Physical agony, enforced by hideous terror, had thrown him into
a convulsion. The father was a hero, when it came to defending his
children. Wrapping a coat about his hands, he picked up the tortured
wisp of puppyhood and carried him from the room into the moonlit
back yard.*

*Next morning the ashman poked curiously at a rumpled and
moveless little bundle of soft brown fur on top of the garbage can. The
father's brave promptitude had saved countless people from being bitten
by a rabid brute. And now he knew from terrible experience that a
collie is an incurably savage dog, and no safe pet for a child.*

*Q. You are always making a case for animals. I would like to ask you
just one thing. Do you believe animals are as important as human beings?*
—I. W., MATTOON, ILL.

A. No, but then I'm human. And therein lies the problem. Albert Schweitzer, for example, believed that an ethical point of view that took in only human life was a logical impossibility. And the basis for our so-called rights, after all, must be impartiality. If you accept the premise that animals do experience both pleasure and pain, and if you further believe that pain is bad, then all pain must be bad—for them as well as for us. Recently, on a trip to the West Coast, I met Vincent Lazara, who teaches a course in moral philosophy at the University of Arizona. One day he asked his students, if they could save only one, which one they would save—the late Rin Tin Tin, or the late Adolph Hitler. About a quarter of the class chose Hitler, whereupon Lazara questioned them. He found that the majority of those who had voted for Hitler did so because they believed that any human life was intrinsically more valuable than any animal life. The reasoning behind this was that only people, and not animals, are capable of rational behavior. Lazara told them that if they were going to swallow that, then they would also have to swallow a bitter pill along with it. This, Professor Lazara pointed out, was that human beings are really only rarely completely rational. So, if the "intrinsic value" of the human life over animal life rests on our rationality, our rights rest on thin grounds—particularly in the case of an Adolf Hitler. As for me, I never took moral philosophy. But I know I'd vote for Rin Tin Tin.